The Lord's Supper

Toward an Ecumenical Understanding of the Eucharist

Philippe Larere, O.P.

translated by
Patrick Madigan, O.S.B.

A Liturgical Press Book

THE LITURGICAL PRESS
Collegeville, Minnesota

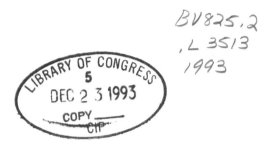
Cover design by Nathan Owen-Block

This book was originally published in French as *L'Eucharistie Repas du Seigneur: Divine Liturgie, Messe et Sainte Cène* by Editions du Lion de Juda/Pneumathèque, La Société des Oeuvres Communautaires, Burtin, 41600 Nouan le Fuzelier, France. Copyright © 1991 Pneumathèque, Société des Oeuvres Communautaires.

Excerpts from the English translation of *The Roman Missal* © 1973, 1985, International Committee on English in the Liturgy, Inc. (ICEL). All rights reserved.

1   2   3   4   5   6   7   8   9

Library of Congress Cataloging-in-Publication Data

Larere, Philippe.
   [Eucharistie, repas du Seigneur. English]
   The Lord's Supper : towards an ecumenical understanding of the Eucharist / Philippe Larere ; translated by Patrick Madigan.
     p.   cm.
   ISBN 0-8146-2226-7
   1. Lord's Supper. 2. Lord's Supper (Liturgy) 3. Lord's Supper and Christian union. 4. Intercommunion. 5. Communicatio in sacris.
I. Title.
BV825.2.L3513   1993
234'.163—dc20

93-

98-10816
CIP

Contents

Foreword

Why yet another book on the "Lord's Supper, the Mass, and Holy Communion"? Have not historians and specialists in the liturgy, biblicists, and theologians as well, already treated this subject many times, some in profound studies and others in introductory works seeking only to communicate the most basic notions? Still, at ecumenical and interconfessional meetings, where the Lord's Supper is frequently celebrated in a gathering composed of Christians from different traditions, one sees Catholics taking Communion without knowing the discipline of their Church or the reasons for it, and Protestants taking the Eucharist without being aware of the nature of the Eucharistic presence the Catholic Church believes in. Evangelicals also, sometimes disobeying their pastors, sometimes at their instigation, come forward to receive the Catholic host. Recognizing the same Lord leads naturally to carrying out similar actions, all admittedly going back to Jesus, but to which the various Churches attach different meanings, without always realizing their significance and importance.

In response to this situation, and out of respect for the Churches and their traditions, this book aims to help Christians to decide either to partake or not to partake in the Lord's Supper, in full recognition of what this action signifies and the proper grounds for doing so, in faithfulness to the beliefs of their own Church, and also showing due respect for those of other Churches. To do this it is necessary to recall the biblical foundations for the Eucharist, to indicate the cultural celebrations derived from the meal celebrated by Jesus the evening before his death. We will describe several developments that occurred in the Eucharist and Holy Communion, before describing the unity, as well as the differences, that characterize the various traditions that celebrate the Lord's Supper.

CHAPTER ONE

The Word of God

ISRAEL WORSHIPS

Who, then, are these nomads in the Egyptian desert, who on a certain evening in spring have strangled young goats and lambs, the most perfect of this year's offspring, to offer them in sacrifice and to eat their flesh? This is a secular custom practiced by almost all nomads in the East, while city-dwellers typically offer the firstfruits of the harvest.

However, on this spring evening, under the reign of Pharoah Ramses II, the Hebrews, descendants of Jacob whose name God himself changed into "Israel" (Gen 32:29), revolt against their Egyptian oppressor who, despite the pestilences which have afflicted him (cf. Exod 7–10), refuses to free them. They follow the command of the Lord passed on to them by their strategist Moses:

> On the tenth of this month [the "month of corn"], let each family take an animal, one per house [a lamb], male and without blemish . . . You shall keep him until the fourteenth day of this month. The entire assembly of the community of Israel will slaughter it at sunset. You will take its blood and smear it on the doorposts and the lintel of the houses where you will eat it. You will consume its flesh that night; you will eat it roasted over a fire with unleavened bread and bitter herbs. . . . Consume it in this way, with your loins girt and sandals on your feet, a staff in your hand. You will eat it in haste. It is the Passover [the passage] of the Lord (Exod 12:3-12).

A final plague will come upon Egypt, but the Hebrews know they will be spared:

> I will traverse the entire country of Egypt on that night, says the Lord. I shall strike every first-born of the land of Egypt, of man and beast alike. . . . The blood will serve as a sign on the houses where you shall be. I will see the blood and pass over you, and the destructive pestilence will not touch you when I strike the land of Egypt. That day will become a memorial for you; from age to age you will celebrate it (Exod 12:12-15).

In that way a religious feast was instituted on the occasion of the Exodus of the Hebrews at the time of their liberation from slavery in the land of Egypt; henceforth it was to be celebrated every year. What kind of celebration are we talking about?

The above text identifies two essential and constitutive elements. First, there is the immolation of a lamb whose blood is supposed to preserve the Hebrews from the vindication of the Lord toward the Egyptians. Following this there is to be a community ritual meal where the guests are clothed for a quick departure and eat the flesh of the lamb, unleavened bread, and bitter herbs, contrasting sharply with the succulent onions to be found in Egypt.

However, this sacrifice and this meal, like all the events in the Old Testament, have a figurative significance: they indicate a reality which is to come.

It is a community celebration strictly limited to the People of God, at the most extended to those who have become naturalized Hebrews, but formally forbidden to all strangers:

> No stranger will eat of it. . . . No guest or mercenary will taste it. . . . The whole community will celebrate it. . . . If a foreigner who has settled among you wishes to celebrate it, let him and every male in his household be circumcised. Then . . . he will be like a native of the country (Exod 12:43-49).

It is also the celebration of the Passover. The Lord passes through Egypt and frees his people, and the Hebrews pass from the status of slaves in Egypt to that of free men in Canaan. They will pass through the cleansing waters of the Red Sea (cf. Exod 14:15-31) and thus will cut themselves off from Egypt. They will pass through the test of the desert to reach the Promised Land.

Consequently it is also a celebration instituted in memory of the deliverance from Egypt: from now on it will take place each year to commemorate this event. "This day will be a memorial for you. You will go on this pilgrimage to celebrate the Lord. From age to age by an unchangeable law, you will do this" (Exod 12:14). It is thus by this feast on this day that the people will invoke the divine name and that God will remember his people according to his words to Moses: "I AM, such is my name, from age to age" (Exod 3:15).

Further, it is a celebration intended to maintain and reaffirm the Covenant of the Lord with his people, pronounced in these words that are repeated frequently throughout: "I will be their God and they will be my people." The annual Passover will be a solemn feast in Jerusalem and will take on its full amplitude at the great moments of the history of Israel. So it was when, after years of idolatry, the kings Ezechias first (cf. 2 Kgs 30:15) and Josiah later (2 Kgs 35) restored the cult of the true God; in the same way, at the consecration of the new Temple in 515 B.C.E., after the exile in Babylon:

> The deported celebrated Passover on the fourteenth day of the first month; inasmuch as the priests together with the Levites were purified, all were pure; they then immolated the Passover for all the deported, for their brothers the priests and for themselves. Thus the sons of Israel, returned from deportation, ate with all those who, around them, had broken with the impurity of the country in order to seek the Lord, the God of Israel (Ezra 6:19-21).

Finally, it is a source of strength, called upon to supply endurance for the journey. "Harried out of Egypt without being able to take their time, [the sons of Israel] did not even take provisions" (Exod 12:39). Nourishment along the way will be delivered through the gift of manna.

> At daybreak a layer of dew covered the ground. As the dew dried, there over the desert floor was something thin as having been grated, something as fine as Wyvern on the ground. The sons of Israel looked at each other and said: "Mân hou?" ["What is it?"], for they did not know what it was. Moses told

them: "It is the bread that the Lord gives you to eat" (Exod 16:13-15).

Once they have reached the Promised Land, this provisioning will end, for they will have no more need for it:

> The sons of Israel camped at Guilgal and prepared the Passover. . . . And they ate the products of the land they were to enter the following day. . . . And the manna ceased. . . There was no more manna for the sons of Israel who ate the produce of the land of Canaan that year (Jos 5:10-13).

At the time of Jesus, Passover was celebrated at home according to a precise ritual which is known to us thanks to a writing from the second century of the common era, the Mishna, which sums up the practices of many centuries (Pesahim 10). We will extract several useful sections from it in the following chapters. The lamb was sacrificed in the afternoon in the Temple (at the hour when *Jesus gave up his spirit*). The meal took place once evening arrived, and was inserted, let us say for simplicity's sake, between two blessings. The first invoked the fruit of the vine and the bread of the earth. The last was longer and gave thanks for the food and for the country, "the land of Israel." The ritual meal was situated between these two moments with a speech by the presider who, referring to the Scriptures, "recalled to memory" the deliverance from Egypt and the arrival in the Promised Land.

At this period there were also other more or less festive religious meals, always following the same form: the consumption of food was punctuated and framed as a whole by blessings.

How did Jesus, on the eve of his death, structure his last meal?

———

SUMMARY: *Israel's Passover is fundamentally made up of a ritual meal involving the eating of a recently slain lamb. At the same time, this feast is rich with divergent characteristics: it is the community celebration of a journey in memory of the deliverance from slavery; it is also nourishment. In the time of Jesus, this ritual was framed between two blessings.*

JESUS WORSHIPS

To understand how Jesus celebrated the Passover during which he instituted the Eucharist and to grasp the significance and the meaning of this action and of his words, we have the Gospels of Matthew, Mark, and Luke and a passage from the First Letter of Paul to the Corinthians. Still, in dealing with these one must take into account that these writings were addressed to a specific audience which already celebrated the Lord's Supper.

The most complete account is that of Luke; it is also the one that most closely resembles the unfolding of the celebration of Passover as it was described at the end of the preceding chapter. For example, Luke admits that a first cup circulated among the guests at the dinner: Jesus

> then received a cup, and after having given thanks he said: "take this and share it among you, for I say unto you: from this time on I shall no longer drink the fruit of the wine until the kingdom of God has come." Then he took the bread and, after having given thanks, he broke it and gave it to them. . . . (Luke 22:17-20).

This corresponds to the first blessing at Jewish meals: "Blessed be you, Lord our God, king of the universe, who gives us this fruit from the vine . . . who makes the earth bring forth bread." And the account ends with the words: "And with the cup, he did the same after the meal . . ." (v. 20), thereby indicating that the meal took place between a first and a second blessing, in accord with Jewish custom which specifies a second blessing toward the conclusion of a meal for the food and for "the land of Israel." Further, three times, specifically: "Take the cup and share it among you" (v. 17); "he gave them (the bread)" (v. 19); "and for the cup he did the same" (v. 20), the narrative insists upon this sharing. Thus, according to Luke, the Lord's Supper is indeed a community meal with a ritual character, the first essential element of Israel's Passover.

Luke (like Mark 14:12 and Matt 26:17) teaches us that before the meal "Jesus sent Peter and John, telling them: 'Go prepare the Passover for us, that we may eat it'" (Luke 22:8). However, today certain exegetes (scholars who study the meaning of texts) contend that Jesus could not have eaten the Passover on the night before his death, for he was condemned "on the day of the Preparation for Passover towards the sixth hour" (John 19:14), that is to say, toward noon: he thus could only have celebrated a farewell meal "in a Passover atmosphere" a farewell meal in a family style or in the manner of a more or less self-conscious groups, as happened at that time; and if Luke, Mark, and Matthew suggest that it was the Passover, this is only to underline their conviction that Jesus was the pascal Lamb.

In this scenario, the meal would certainly not have consisted of the meat of a lamb. However, Jesus's words: "This is my Body given for you . . . . This cup is the new Covenant in my blood which will be poured out for you" (vv. 19 & 20) suggest that the authentic Lamb of the Passover is the Person of Christ who will be sacrificed the following day on the cross. The only thing that remains is to know what meaning we should attach to the word "is": does it assert an identity (as it was generally understood to do before the Protestant Reformation), or is it only a metaphor? Because this question has given rise to such disagreement between the Churches, it is a topic for a later chapter. These words equally suggest a lamb, the second essential element to a Jewish Passover.

Thus, as for the principal characteristics of this Passover, both are present in this account: a meal reserved exclusively for certain guests: "he gave it to them" (v. 19), that is, to those present, not to others. Further, it is the celebration of a journey, a passage—and how! It was no longer only the movement through the desert from Egypt to Canaan. Rather, it consists in the Passion of the Christ, the Anointed One, who will pass from this world where sin reigns to the plenitude of the Kingdom of God. It is a memorial: that is made clear in explicit terms: "Do this in memory of me" (v. 19). The memorial of the deliverance from Egypt thereby becomes a memorial of the Passion completing this deliverance, indeed of which it was the figure. It is even necessary to translate: "Do this in my name," for in French to "memorialize" is to remember, but here it is rather a question of "invoking the name" in conformity with the biblical passage: "THE LORD, that is my name forever, that is my memorial from age to age'' (Exod 3:15). For the name of the Lord designates the very person of the Lord: ''Father, glorify your name''. . . . (John 12:28). To know him is to find oneself in his presence; to invoke him is to enter into communion with him.

Another characteristic: this is a celebration of the Covenant. This is so indeed, because the first Covenant between God and his People is not abolished. It is in fact extended to this second and ''new Covenant in my blood'' (v. 20), which frees from sin as the blood of the lambs deflected the revenge of the Lord and which is the gift of divine life in return for faith; this Covenant from now on is sealed in the blood of Christ.

As for its character as nourishment, this is not explicit in Luke, but it is in Matthew's account: ''Take and eat'' (26:26). Certainly he is speaking about food; but what type? Physical? Spiritual? And what is there to say about it? Since the various Churches are not in agreement on this topic, this question is taken up later.

Mark's and Matthew's accounts, with the exception of the commands ''Take'' in Mark and ''Take and eat'' in Matthew, scarcely differ in essentials from that of Luke. However, one should point out that Luke situates the institution of the Eucharist within the framework of the Jewish ritual, while Mark and Matthew develop it in accord with the practice of the Christian celebration, where it took place ''during a meal'' (Mark 14:22; Matt 26:26) at the time when their texts were written. Jesus there declares, as in Luke: ''From this time on I will no longer drink of the fruit of the vine'' until his return (Luke 22:18; Mark 14:25; Matt 26:29). For the reason, that is, that they have in mind the Christian cult and not the format of the Jewish meal, Mark and Matthew prefer the expression ''blood . . . poured out for all,'' that is, for the many (cf. Isa 53:12), the totality of humans. And Matthew adds: ''for the forgiveness of sins'' (v. 27), thereby making specific the meaning to be attached to Jesus's death.

What's more, beyond this conformity of Jesus's last meal with the celebration of the Jewish Passover, by choosing bread and wine as elements for the institution of the new Covenant, Jesus indicated the link between this covenant and creation:

is not this bread, the symbol of earthly nourishment earned by man "by the sweat of his brow" (Gen 3:19), fundamentally a gift from the Creator? And does not this wine, associated with the miracle at Cana carried out by Jesus for the faith of the people (cf. John 2:1-11), proclaim better than water the excellence of this gift?

Paul's account is the oldest (from the middle of the first century, while the three evangelists quoted are from about twenty years later). It is first of all an occasional piece addressed to the Corinthian community, where the Lord's Supper was being disrupted, rather than being celebrated with sharing and dignity. Comparing it to the Lukan account to which it parallels, it has certain emphases: one should pay attention to the words and actions of the Lord: "Here is what I received from the Lord, and what I passed on to you" (1 Cor 11:23); the declaration of the Lord's return is preceded by the mention of his death: "You announce the death of the Lord until he comes" (v. 26); one must be dignified and conscious of the reality one is approaching. Thus one should not take Communion unworthily or without proper awareness, for one risks thereby various punishments which an earlier conversion could have avoided (cf. vv. 27-33). This account makes no mention of a first circulation of the cup, but in an earlier passage, written to the same occasion, Paul asks: "The cup of blessing that we bless, is it not a sharing in the blood of Christ?" (1 Cor 10:16).

This background of religious meals in Israel for the celebration of the Lord's Supper appears elsewhere in Luke's writings. In the well-known account of the disciples on the road to Emmaus (cf. Luke 24), the Resurrected One unpacks the meaning of the Scriptures just as he did in the synagogues, before taking bread, pronouncing the blessing, breaking it, and giving it to them. In the same way do we not have, several years after the ascension, a similar cult of the Word and of Communion when Luke writes: "Then when we were reunited to break bread, Paul, who was to depart the following day, addressed these words to the brothers" (Acts 20:7)?

From the weight of these texts, one should notice that the structure of the unfolding of the religious meal in Israel was retained in the Lord's Supper, especially in the four principal acts of Jesus: taking, blessing, breaking, and sharing. Continuously down to our own time (with exceptions only for rather recent deviations in some Churches), this structure and these elements have been perpetuated in the celebration of the Eucharist and Holy Communion. The sequence is cultic: first the bread and wine are prepared; there follows a prayer of thanksgiving into which the account of the institution is inserted; and the celebration concludes with the "breaking of the bread" (an expression used by Luke in Acts 2:42) and the distribution of Communion.

SUMMARY: *The Lord's Supper completes the Passover of Israel, which prefigured it. They have the same essential elements: a ritual common meal and the presence of the Lamb (but now sacrificed the next day on the cross). They also have the same characteristics: a community (of the baptized); a transition (with the promise of the return of the Lord, prefigured by the entry into the Promised Land); they are both a memorial; they both involve a renewal of the Covenant; they are both food (here "spiritual and physical," on condition that we agree how to understand these words). What's more, the words and actions of Jesus, pronounced and carried out within this framework, are integral to the celebrations of the Church: the Word of God preceding the preparation of the gifts of bread and wine, a great prayer of praise with the account of the Institution, the breaking of the bread, and Communion.*

JESUS TEACHES

Before discussing the evolution of the Lord's Supper through the centuries, it is useful to consider what the Apostle John says about it. His Gospel is late (end of the first century) and does not have an Institutional narrative, but rather a "discourse on the Bread of Life" (in chapter 6) and the episode of the washing of the feet which he locates "before the feast of Passover . . . during a meal" (cf. 13:1-20). In what ways does this

Gospel confirm or complete, or perhaps on the contrary, weaken or contradict the earlier accounts we have considered?

They reflect different oral traditions: while the other three evangelists and the Apostle Paul emphasize the cultic act carried out by Jesus during his Last Supper, John is more interested in recalling the foundation for this act, that is, the Love of God and of neighbor: "Before the feast of Passover, Jesus, knowing that his hour had come, the hour when he was to pass from this world to the Father, he who had loved his own who are in the world, loved them to the end. During a meal . . . Jesus got up from the table, put aside his garment and took a towel with which he began to wash the feet of his disciples and to dry them with the cloth at his belt" (John 13:1-6). And Jesus explains the meaning of his action thus to his Apostles: "Do you understand what I have done for you?. . . if I have washed your feet, I the Lord and Teacher, you also must wash the feet of one another; for it is an example" (in the strong sense of this word: a prototype, a command, an order) "that I have given to you; what I have done for you, do you also for one another" (John 13:12-16). Such is the lesson of the washing of the feet; Jesus thus expresses in a different way than his words over the bread and wine his love for people, which he manifested through his life and which he carried to its extreme by his Passion and death on the cross.

This episode begins the long exchange between Jesus and his apostles on the eve of his Passion, which constitutes his spiritual testament and whose theme is mutual love. "I give you a new commandment: love one another. By this all will recognize that you are my disciples: by the love which you have for one another" (John 13:34-36). During this final encounter, a metaphor, that of the vine and its branches, becomes the basis for this teaching: "Remain in me as I remain in you. Just as the branch, if it is separated from the vine, cannot produce fruit of itself, you also will not bear fruit if you do not remain in me. I am the vine, you are the branches . . . ." (John 15:4) In this way John accents the fruit of the celebration of the Last Supper, that is, the Love for God and for our neighbor.

But to discover the nature of this life-giving nourishment that he gives his disciples, we must look at chapter 6 of his Gospel, where Jesus says explicitly:

"It is I who am the bread of life" (v. 35); "I am the bread of life" (v. 48); "I am the bread come down from heaven. The person who eats this bread will live for eternity. And the bread which I give you, it is my flesh, given for the life of the world." (v. 51): "If you do not eat of the flesh of the Son of man and if you do not drink his blood, you will not have life in you. The person who eats my flesh and drinks my blood has life eternal. . . . For my flesh is real food, and my blood real drink. The person who eats my flesh and drinks my blood remains in me and I in them. . . . The person who eats this bread will live for eternity" (vv. 53-59).

This long discourse (cf. vv. 26-65) which follows the signs of the multiplication of loaves and the walking on the water has provoked numerous commentaries with different points of view. Not to digress long upon it, and in line with the concerns of this study, it is a matter of the person of Jesus offering up his divine life. But what type of food are we speaking of: is this the bread of the Eucharist, or is it rather the bread of the Word? In either case, we should not lose sight of John's intention in writing his Gospel: these signs, he reports at the end, have been gathered together in this book "so that you may believe that Jesus is the Christ, the Son of God; and that, by believing, you may have life in his name" (John 20:31).

That this food is that of the Word leading to faith is clearly affirmed three times: "It is I who am the bread of life: the person who comes to me will not taste hunger; the person who believes in me will never be thirsty" (v. 35); "the person who believes in life eternal" (v. 47); "It is the Spirit who gives life, the flesh is useless" (v. 63). This interpretation appears to rest upon at least two assumptions. First, that the discourse is like a parable, that is, a comparison where what is described is not simply an illustration but uncovers the meaning: the bread of life should be understood here as the person of Jesus attained by faith, an interpretation which the verses quoted confirm. Thus Jesus can proclaim: "I am the Bread of life" as elsewhere: "I am the sheep's gate" (John 10:7). In line with this, and as a second point, this interpretation supposes that these three verses explain the words of Jesus which, in the last analysis, because they were tough, hard to swallow, "difficult" (v. 60), caused most of his hearers to leave, and that they thus provide the key to the entire discourse. In short, this food is completely spiritual.

That this food is that of the Eucharist seems clearly stated in verses 48 to 59, whose essential parts were quoted above. An interpretation from this point of view takes account of the context: after the miracle of the multiplication of the loaves (cf. John 6:1-16), Jesus addresses a crowd which is experiencing hunger and thirst, and he intends to lead them, with this as a basis, to desire the divine nourishment which is nothing less than his person: "It is not because you have seen signs that you seek me, but because you have eaten bread until you were satisfied. You must strive to obtain not a food that passes away, but the food that leads to life eternal. . . ." We see that this interpretation is not that of a parable, but of an affirmation: to have the divine life, you must eat my flesh and drink my blood. The allusion to the manna supports this, for it recalls the now out of date figure anticipating the present reality: "In the desert your fathers ate manna, and they died. The bread that descends from heaven is such that the person who eats it will not die." (vv. 49, 50). Finally Jesus expresses himself clearly: "My flesh is real food and my blood is real drink" (v. 55); the Greek word used should really be translated as "genuine," and means that it truly nourishes, while above (cf. v. 32) John uses a word that should be translated "truly," to distinguish this bread from the manna which was nothing but a kind of white dew. Such a reading presents a revelation of the mystery (otherwise expressed, of the hidden reality) of the Eucharist. It recognizes that Jesus expresses the necessity of eating "his flesh and blood," otherwise expressed, of appropriating his person (or more exactly of being appropriated by his person, for he is the Living One). No less does it affirm that this mysterious consumption takes place in a spiritual manner and can only come about through faith: that is the thrust of verses 35, 47, and 63, which establish the spiritual interpretation of this passage. From this perspective, we are dealing with a sacrament, a visible sign that opens up to us and makes accessible the invisible reality which it signifies. In short, this food is simultaneously spiritual and physical.

Beyond these two possible interpretations of the text, and having taken account of the fact that John's Gospel intends to lead its readers to faith in Jesus as the Savior (cf. 20:31), the intention of this text is to call us to believe in it. "You must strive to obtain . . . the food that the Son of Man will give you."—God made man (v. 27); "The bread I give you is my flesh for the life of the world"—to save humankind (v. 51). We are thus led from the reality of this mysterious food to another reality which far transcends it, specifically, salvation in the person of Jesus Christ, whom we must join. But that is precisely the way a symbol operates, for in a symbol the visible reality is available to all, while the represented reality depends on each person individually. Is not this symbolic interpretation compatible with the two preceding interpretations?

SUMMARY: *Far from weakening the accounts of the institution of the Eucharist in the Synoptic Gospels and in Paul, John's Gospel underlines the foundation of this institution, specifically, the love of God and of our neighbor. However, the discourse on the Bread of life is open to different interpretations—purely spiritual or more sacramental—but first and above all "symbolic," in the sense that the purpose of a symbol is to lead one from a given reality to another reality that each can encounter for themselves. Taking account of the manifest intention of John's Gospel, it is clear that this other reality is nothing other than the person of Jesus the Savior, whom each person is then free to accept or refuse.*

CHAPTER TWO

Across the Centuries

THE FIRST CHRISTIAN MEALS

"Do this in memory of me," said Jesus, during his last meal after having taken the bread, blessed and broken it, and before passing it around and blessing the cup; it was obviously a religious meal such as was common among the Jews at that time—in the traditional view a Passover, but perhaps also a "fellowship meal" around Jesus. Once risen, he himself performed the same gestures on the road to Emmaus in front of the two disciples who recognized him through this: "When he was at table with them, he took bread, pronounced the words of blessing, broke it and gave it to them. Then their eyes were opened and they recognized him, and then he vanished from their sight" (Luke 24:30-31). How, then, did the first disciples of Jesus carry this on in their communities? What form did they follow in their celebrations? If Jewish meals provided a framework for imitation for the Last Supper of Jesus, which were they? Here we must consult the Acts of the Apostles.

The Jews of that time practiced various religious meals either in the family or among friends. There were the purification meals for the membership of different organizations. Thus, for example, the Essenes, who have left traces of a community on the shore of the Dead Sea at Qumran, performed a number of ablutions. Also the Pharisees made great efforts to observe scrupulously the prescriptions of the Law, preferred to stay apart, separated from the impure world, a bit in the manner of a sect, etc. There were also the solemn festivities at the principal feasts of the year: at Passover to offer the first fruits, at

Pentecost to celebrate the harvest, at the feast of Tabernacles at the time of the vintage, etc.

Above all there were the meals which marked the daily and weekly rhythms of the people, and which consequently were more numerous. Each day the family came together to pray and to eat kosher (that is, with the exclusion of certain culinary preparations disallowed by the rituals) and in abstaining also from certain specified foods said to be impure; it is in this way that one prepared the "bowl of the poor," a type of food that was suited for the needy and those in flight. Each week on the eve of the Sabbath (the day of rest), the community came together in the same way; it was then that one prepared the "basket of the poor" for the most deprived and the widows. Besides these family and group meals, there were various services for mutual aid. It seems likely that there were charity meals, especially among the Diaspora, the Jewish communities scattered throughout the Roman Empire, at which funds were raised for the relief of other communities in need.

In such a context, the first of Jesus's disciples, who were simply one more religious association among the Jews similar to many others, with the exception that they believed in the resurrection of Jesus, gathered together among themselves and even lived and thus ate together "faithful to the teaching of the apostles and to the fraternal community, to the breaking of the bread and to prayer, . . . they were united and held all things in common" (Acts 2:42-45). The Book of Acts also reports that a certain group of the widows "were overlooked in the daily service," (Acts 6:1), that the group gathered on the day of the Lord's resurrection "the first day of the week . . . to break bread" (Acts 20:7). Without even invoking the passage in Paul's letters which provided the occasion for an account of the institution of the Lord's Supper (cf. 1 Cor 11:17-33), these texts are sufficient to show that the first Christian communities came together in the same way as the neighboring Jewish communities and that during these meetings where a meal was shared a "Memorial of the Lord" was conducted in accord with Jesus's command.

This custom was in fact the point of departure for an evolution of the Lord's Meal which culminated in our contemporary celebrations of the Eucharist and Lord's Supper, by structuring these around the principal actions that Jesus carried out during his last meal: taking, blessing, breaking, and sharing.

Before examining this development, we must understand how the community was built up around this Jesus who was no longer there, but who each of the participants nevertheless held firmly in faith to be alive: he is absent, and yet, there is no doubt about it, he is present. It is important to say this in advance, for the celebration of the Lord's Supper by these communities rapidly became the origin and source of growth for faith in Jesus resurrected; as a consequence, it is the site of the production of the Gospel texts. We should not imagine the witnesses of the words and deeds of Jesus like reporters relating bald facts which the communities later flesh out: that could have produced only a "tall tale" about Jesus. Instead, there was a religious experience based on the faith of the believers, beginning with that of the first witnesses who heard and saw Jesus resurrected, those who had "eaten and drunk with him" (cf. Acts 10:39-41). During these meetings, in the course of a religious meal, the amazing words and deeds of Jesus were brought forth, his crowning deed was reenacted "in his memory." In such a way there would have developed the awareness that he was manifesting himself. In this way the believing community edified itself by speaking, doing, and sharing, by the Word and the Deed, around this Bread of the Word and of the "Memorial."

Since Jesus, recognized as present through the faith of the believers, physically is absent, who, then, will "take, bless, break, and give"?

In a Jewish meal celebrated in the home, the father of the family or the master of the house is the presider. It is he who takes the cup and the bread, pronounces the blessing, breaks the bread, distributes it and normally explains the meaning of his words and actions. If we are dealing with a more solemn feast, there are also servants who portion out the gifts and the result of the collection for beggars, those in need in the community, widows, and guests in transit. There are also servants of the word who comment upon the Scriptures, who teach or exhort. These functions were formally recognized and divided during the religious services at the synagogue: servants of the written word such as doctors of the Law and scribes who present the Scriptures, teach it, interpret it and discuss its applications; servants of the word who are preachers, embellishing and spinning out marvelous tales, or "midrash," to give a more profound interpretation to the biblical text.

In the Christian meal there is similarly someone who presides: it is the one who takes the cup and the bread, pronounces the words of institution, breaks the bread and distributes it; that is to say, in a single and more telling description, it is the one who brings about the "sharing." (In the first century historians used the term "Christian meal" to distinguish from "Jewish meal," which was always more or less a holy event. Here "Christian meal" does not refer to a simple agape, but to the meal of Christ's resurrection, the Eucharist.) There are also table servants as well, a service of which the Twelve were quick to dismiss: "It is not proper that we neglect the word of God for table service. Look, then, among yourselves, brothers, for seven men of good reputation, filled with the Spirit and with wisdom, and we will charge them with this function. As for ourselves, we shall continue seeing to the prayer and the service of the Word" (Acts 6:2-5).

Further, this service of the Word will itself soon be divided among the membership: "When you have come together, let one of you sing a canticle, another instruct the others or bring forth a revelation, another speak in tongues, or interpret such speaking" (1 Cor 14:26-27). And the single Word of God thus divided will be controlled by those who have proper authority, that is, by those who have heard it and live from it and are thus apt to judge the conformity of these words with the Word of God: "Examine everything with attention, retain what is good" (1 Thess 5:21). However, there emerges one major difference between the Jewish and the Christian meal. In the first, the word of the presider and of the other servants is always a word or an explanation about an event or persons, and the servants distribute the gifts on behalf of the community. In the second, the presider takes the place of the Lord Jesus and speaks and acts "in his memory," "in his name"; the table servers and the other servants of the Word also take his place in distributing the gifts and doubtless also in distributing the bread. At this point it is no longer a matter of a word *about* Jesus or of a giving on his behalf; rather, it is the Word of Jesus, and it is *he* who speaks; it is Jesus's Gift, and it is *he* who serves. Was it not thus already with the meal of those walking on the road to Emmaus: in speaking about him, he himself spoke; after having broken the bread, he distributed it himself, before the two disciples recognized him in this breaking of the bread (cf. Luke 24). Thus, the real presider who speaks, blesses, breaks the bread, and gives it is Jesus himself.

This same Jesus is operative in the Christian meal in a different way than in the Passover meal of the Jews. In the latter there were those who sacrificed, the priests of the tribe of Levi, and victims, the lambs, who in Jesus's time were slaughtered in the courtyard of the Temple before the evening meal of the families or associations. Here, however, one and the same Jesus, present in the role of presider at the meal, will offer himself in the same terms as at his last meal on the eve of his death. "This is my body given for you. Do this in memory of me. . . This cup is the new covenant in my blood poured out for you" (Luke 22:19-21). Now, these words of Jesus have established not only a precise connection, but also a still contemporary link between the supper and the cross. On Calvary he was sacrificed, but he was himself the one carrying out the sacrifice: "My life, no one takes it from me, but I give it up myself" (John 10:18). Jesus sacrificed himself in this unique offering that need not be repeated, that eclipses, completes, brings to their culmination all the previous sacrifices, and renders fruitless any other that might come later. At the cenacle he symbolized through his words and deeds what he was about to accomplish the following day. This symbolic action is an anticipation, and this anticipation is an actualization of what his sacrifice on the cross means.

Again, what do we understand by "symbol," "sacrifice," and "actualization"? In its primary sense, a symbol is the showing forth of one reality by another. The cenacle act, then, is the act through which Jesus explained his sacrifice on the cross. As for sacrifice, it is the act through which one makes amends to a deity whom he or she has offended by being deprived of something and offering it to the divinity. Thus Jesus offers the Father his own life out of love for us, so that the Father may extend to us the gift of his love, in the face of which sin was an obstacle. Finally, actualization is nothing other than the insertion (and not the repetition) of a given event at another moment of time, such that for Jesus to actualize the cross, is to render the deed present at the moment of the celebration of his Last Supper. Since, therefore, the cenacle where Jesus speaks and performs on the eve of his death symbolizes and actualizes the sacrifice of the cross, Jesus is present there as a sacrifice, of course, not physically, but mysteriously, as the Eastern tradition puts it (or sacramentally, in the language of the West).

But what about the kind of Lord's Supper that would be celebrated by his disciples after the resurrection? At the very least, such a celebration would have recalled the last meal of Jesus where he revealed himself. But to stop at that point is to hold oneself to a literal and fundamentalistic interpretation of the texts; more precisely, it is not to take into account the event of the resurrection itself. For in fact there is more; because Jesus risen is from now on always and forever to be found in the world as well, as he himself said: "I am with you all days, even to the end of the world" (Matt 28:20), because the community gathered together for this meal believes in the actual presence of the Risen one.

Deriving sustenance from this presence, the Christian meal is *par excellence* the moment and the occasion where his disciples not only recall that Jesus formerly revealed himself through the bread and wine in a disposition of sacrifice. More importantly they are on the point of recognizing him *again*, following the example of the disciples on the road to Emmaus, with their eyes of faith, as being he who manifests himself in our presence symbolically in the condition in which he found himself as the unique sacrifice on the cross, without having to repeat this or add anything to it. In this way the Christian meal expresses day by day all that Jesus accomplished (more precisely, intended and carried out) during his last meal.

There remains one final aspect of the Christian meal that we could not treat fully before we had shown how Jesus allows himself to be recognized and extends himself through these actions of taking, blessing, breaking, and sharing. This is that the Christian meal is the reunion of a brotherly community. It was on the command of the Lord that ''the entire community of Israel'' celebrated Passover through the means of ''one animal per family, or one for each house'' (Exod 12:1-4). It was by the order of Jesus and because of profound desire that the Twelve were invited to this last meal. ''Go prepare the Passover for us, that we may eat it. . . . I have strongly desired to eat this Passover with you'' (Luke 22:8, 15). It was to be reunited around their Lord that the first disciples ''of one mind'' (Acts 2:46) ''were attentive to the fraternal communion (in Greek, the *koinônia*), to the breaking of the bread'' (v. 42).

This group meal is at the same time an occasion for mutual service, where the presence and action of Jesus who offers himself and allows himself to be recognized unites those present as strongly with one another as with himself: ''Because there is one bread, we are all one body; for we all share in this one bread'' (1 Cor 10:17). The gathering of the community becomes a reunion in the Love of the Lord by all believers, the place where a real ''sharing'' in this Love takes place. Unfortunately, the various Churches understand differently the connection of cause and effect between the sharing of all in the Body of Christ and the convocation of a ''gathered community,'' the *Ecclesia*, the Church. Is it merely a matter of performing together a fraternal action, or of replenishing oneself for the daily exertions of existence? Or rather, does not this celebrating community, by thus gathering around the Lord from whom it derives its life, form the Church—but if so, how? We will comment on this topic later.

―――――――

SUMMARY: *After Jesus's resurrection, his disciples continue to celebrate his last meal following his command, ''Do this in memory of me,'' and do so within the framework of a Jewish religious meal which fuses together simultaneously a sharing in the repast and a sharing of goods. This is not simply to memorialize someone who has been lost, but rather to gather together in Love around the Risen one who continues to reach out and be recognized. Thus, a community united in his Person is—in a word, a Church.*

THE EASTERN TRADITION

Beyond the first century, with customs inherited from the synagogue practice, the form of the Lord's Supper probably remained essentially the same. The service would include, on the one hand, hymns and psalms, readings and a homily, and on the other prayers (thanksgiving and petition) around the bread and wine. But throughout the East these elements evolved in time and took on different forms in different locations.

In the second and third centuries the celebrations moved from private homes into public buildings (we would call them municipal halls today) called basilicas and used for trials or public gatherings. To arrange it for a Christian worship, one could use the throne of the presider and simply set up a rostrum (an ambo) for the readings and a table (an altar) for the celebration of the meal.

We do not know a lot about the pattern of the celebration during this period. However, a catechism from the very beginning of the second century, the *Didaché,* contains prayers in use at the Lord's Supper:

> Here is how you will give thanks. First, over the cup: "We give you thanks, our Father, for the holy vine of David your servant, which you have allowed us to discover through Jesus your servant; to you be glory for the ages." Then over the bread that has been broken: "We give you thanks, our Father, for life and for the knowledge which you have allowed us to discover through Jesus your servant; to you be glory for ever. Just as this broken bread that was scattered over the mountains and hillsides has been gathered together to make one loaf, so may your Church be gathered from the far corners of the earth into your Kingdom. For to you belongs glory and power through Jesus Christ, forever and ever." Let no one eat or drink from your Eucharist, except those who have been baptized in the name of the Lord. . . . (*Didaché* 9).

And the text continues:

> After having eaten, this is how you will give thanks: "We give
> you thanks, holy Father, for your holy name which you have
> placed in our hearts. . . . Remember your Church, Lord, pre-
> serve her from every evil, and make her perfect in your love.
> And gather her from the four corners of the world into the King-
> dom which you have prepared for her, this Church which you
> have rendered holy" (10).

Further on, we read again:

> As you gather together on Sunday, the day of the Lord, break
> bread and give thanks after having confessed your sins. . . .
> But if some one has a difference with his neighbor, he should
> not join you until the two have been reconciled (14).

Another early record of the celebration of the Lord's Supper is this police report from the year 112 addressed by the
governor of Bithynia, Pliny the Younger, to the Emperor Tra-
jan, where one reads that the Christians "customarily gather
together on a fixed day, before the sun comes up, to sing back
and forth among themselves a hymn to Christ as to a God. . .;
after these rites are completed, they usually separate and then
come together again to take some food which, according to report, is ordinary and innocent. . . ." (R. Cabie, *The Church
at Prayer: The Eucharist* [Collegeville: The Liturgical Press,
1986]).

Beginning in the fourth century, we have more ample
documentation; the variety is impressive. An *anaphora* (the
name for a Eucharistic prayer in the East) said to be from Ad-
daï and Mari goes back to the third century and comes from
Edessa in eastern Syria (today Urfa in Turkey). The manu-
scripts, apparently much later, take the form of a praise
and *anamnesis* (a prayer recalling the death, resurrection, and
ascension of the Lord), which may have included an account
of the Institution. A little later from Antioch came the Syrian
anaphora of the Twelve Apostles: a preface of praise with the
"Holy, Holy, Holy," an Institution narrative, the *anamnesis*,
epiclesis (an address to the Holy Spirit to bless the offerings of

bread and wine), a prayer for the universal Church, and an intercession of the saints.

These assorted texts allow us to sketch the probable evolution of the parts of the celebration. The "memorial" was part of the meal as long as the Christians were still regularly attending services in the Temple at Jerusalem. A bit later the meal (now doubtless a simple *agape*) was separated from the liturgical celebration which had borrowed from the customs of the synagogue: to these, prayers, readings, and sayings were added the "take, bless, break, and distribute" in memory of Jesus. Doubtless there were hardly any strict formulations, but rather an oral transmission which was flexible and creative. This led to invoking the death, resurrection, and ascension of the Lord. Hence there developed a prayer of anamnesis, as well as the need to implore the Spirit of Jesus, who alone is capable of allowing the Absent one who is always present to the eyes of faith to operate through the words and deeds of the celebrants.

The East came to know more than a hundred anaphoras (Eucharistic prayers) and a diversified liturgical style. This is to be explained through the spread of the Church through these regions during the first centuries. Antioch and Alexandria, later Constantinople (Byzantium), and finally Jerusalem, became distinct patriarchates, each with its own customs and way of celebrating the liturgy. This style extended to the local Churches that fell under their impulse and which in turn modified the liturgy to function in their particular situations. Antioch, where the language of celebration was Greek, succeeded in spreading its style throughout Syria (more or less the entire modern Near East); then a Syriac rite developed in the Aramean dialect. The same process occurred in Persia and Asia. Alexandria developed a liturgy in Egypt and gave birth to both a Coptic and an Ethiopian rite.

Constantinople, having become the "New Rome" in 381, spread the liturgical style of St. Basil and St. John Chrysostom. Jerusalem influenced the Armenian rite. After the Council of Chalcedon in 451, a local Church separated, later giving rise to the Jacobites, from the name of the founder Jacob Bar Adaï, while the Melkites (from the Aramean: *melek*, prince) remained faithful to the emperor's Church. In the following century, Christians originally from Antioch, to escape vexations from the Jacobites and Greeks, emigrated to the high places of Lebanon and ended up forming the Maronite Church (from the name of the local ascetic Mar Maron), etc.

The advantage of having a plurality of anaphoras is that each one can be specific and correspond to local customs or express the particular emotion of a feast. The Byzantine liturgy only has two such anaphoras: that of St. Basil, longer and more solemn, and that of St. John Chrysostom, the more commonly used and international. The latter was picked up by the Bulgars, the Russians, the Serbs, etc, and today is used in both the Orthodox Churches and those Eastern Churches in union with Rome, with a few exceptions. How did it develop to its contemporary form?

This "divine liturgy" (the expression chosen to designate the Lord's Supper in the Byzantine rite) includes, like the others, two parts: a first called the "*synaxis* (assembly) of the catechumens," for the latter and those preparing for baptism were admitted to this part, and a second called the "eucharistic synaxis" or "liturgy of the faithful" reserved for those already baptized. The details of the liturgy of St. John Chrysostom are described later. Here we will highlight certain elements which developed over time.

From the beginning of the sixth century, the synaxis of the catechumens included two successive introductions: first an invocation called the *Trisagion:* "O Holy God, Holy and Strong, immortally Holy, have mercy on us"; then a chant for entering in procession:

> Only Son and Word of God, Immortal One who, for our salvation, deigned to take flesh through the holy Mother of God, Mary ever virgin; who, without undergoing change, still became man, was crucified, Christ God, who by your death has vanquished death; You, One of the Persons of the Holy Trinity, one in glory with the Father and the Holy Spirit, save us.

The proclamation of the Gospel is marked by lights and incense as well as with acclamations of "Alleluia" to indicate the coming of Christ. Beginning in the eighth century, a kiss of the gospel book is introduced. This is the origin of the ritual called the ''Small Entrance.''

There follows a universal prayer, that is, a series of prayer intentions for the Church and the world in the form of a litany to which the assembly answers *''Kyrie eleison*—Have mercy on us.'' This practice dates back to the fourth century.

The Eucharistic synaxis also has several distinctive elements. The preparation of the bread and wine, placed on a small table to one side and carried to the altar by the deacons, develops during the seventh century or perhaps earlier into a solemn procession that will become in time the ''Great Entrance.'' The Institution Narrative includes some words that are not to be found in the gospel accounts: ''having taken bread into his sacred hands, pure and without blemish.'' The anamnesis adopts a symbolic language: ''We offer you things which come from you,'' but the epiclesis employs more concrete expressions: ''Transform this bread into the precious body of Christ and this cup into the blood of Christ.'' And the doxology (the concluding prayer to the glory of God), in a way distinctive to the entire East (in contrast to the Western formulations), mentions the Father, the Son, and the Spirit without indicating the order or succession between them.

The Communion also has several particularities. The ''Our Father'' is recited before the breaking of the bread, contrary to the usage of the other Eastern rites. Hot water is poured into the chalice so that the heat may fill the cup the way the Spirit gives life to the faithful: this is the *zéon*. Before communion, the faithful are invited to bow: this custom comes from Antioch. They hear the spoken words: *Tà àgia tois àgiois*—''holy things to holy people,'' so that ''each one may examine him or her self before taking this bread and drinking from this cup'' (1 Cor 11:28). They answer: ''Only one is holy, only one is Lord, Jesus Christ, to the glory of God the Father''; this is a custom common to the Eastern Churches. They take both the body and the blood of Christ.

Also of course, in case there are several priests, they celebrate together around the same table.

223776

SUMMARY: *The Eastern tradition of the Lord's Supper developed from the customs in Antioch and Alexandria following the earliest Christian meals. It rapidly became more complex and diverse as the Church expanded and resulted in several distinct Eucharistic prayers. Today, however, almost the entire Christian East employs the divine liturgy of St. John Chrysostom. See chapter 3.*

THE WESTERN TRADITION

How did progress occur from the first Christian meals to what the Roman tradition will later call the Mass? It is difficult to uncover what happened in the first centuries; however, a text from the first half of the second century that describes the celebration on the Lord's day:

> On the day of the Sun, all those in the cities or in the country-side come together at the same spot. They read, as much as the weather will permit, the records of the apostles or the prophetic writings. Then the reader stops and the presider arises to give an exhortation and to invite the company to follow the beautiful examples that have just been given. At that point everyone arises and the prayers begin. Finally . . . when the prayers are finished, bread, wine, and water are brought forward; the presider prays over them and gives thanks for as long as he can; the people respond by acclamation "Amen." Each one receives their part in the eucharistic elements, and a part is sent to those absent through the ministry of the deacons.

And the text continues: "Those who are rich and who wish to, contribute, each as much as he has decided; the collection is gathered and given over to the presider, who makes sure that it is used for those who are in need" (Justin, *Apologies*, 1, 67). Thus, at that time there was already, as in our time, a liturgy of the Word with readings from the Old Testament (the prophetic writings) and from the New (the accounts from the apostles), as well as a homily (exhortation); and a liturgy of the Eucharist with the presider, his assistants (deacons, ministers to distribute the Eucharistic elements), and the assembly which answers "Amen." We also find in this text mention of an offering for those in need in terms close to those used today in many evangelical Churches, where "each one is invited to give according to his heart."

Equally interesting are these lines from the same author:

> We call this food the Eucharist and no one may share in it who does not believe in the truth we teach, if they have not received the washing for the forgiveness of sins and new birth, and if they do not live according to the precepts of Christ. . . . The food that has been consecrated through the prayer and words coming from Him, through the assimilation of which our blood and bodies are nourished, are the flesh and blood of the incarnate Jesus. This is our teaching (*idem,* 66).

Thus, in order to consume this Passover, one must believe, have been baptized, and lead a Christian life. The Eucharist is an assimilation into the very flesh and blood of Christ, that is to say, into his person.

Another ancient text, this time from the first half of the third century, is the so-called Apostolic Tradition, from the priest Hippolytus of Rome. It presents a Eucharistic liturgy with thanksgiving, an institution narrative, anamnesis, epiclesis, and doxology punctuated with "Amens." The most recent liturgical reform in the Catholic Church adopted closely one of these Eucharistic prayers.

The Apostolic Tradition was probably not written in Latin but rather in Greek, and the part containing the Eucharistic prayer is only known to us in Arab and Ethiopian translations. This shows its influence even in the East. However, it was not universally followed, even at Rome; moreover, Hippolytus himself tells us that his proposed text should not be "recited by heart" (Apostolic Tradition, 9). The creativity of the Churches thus counts for much of the diversification in the rites: the practice at Milan is not that of Rome and does not borrow from the tradition of Hippolytus. What can we say about these rites distinct from that of Rome and which become common in the West?

There is the Ambrosian rite of the Church of Milan. There were certain practices in France and others in Spain whose distinctness lasted through the Arab domination. There were also rites particular to the various religious orders: Carthusians, Dominicans, etc. In all the essentials, the structure of the celebration was similar to that of Rome, but it was possible to have differences that are important for the rite of one or the other group. For example, the Carthusians and Dominicans did not prepare the bread and wine at the time that it was done in the Roman rite, and the prayer that accompanies this action is less elaborate. Even in the same region there were different customs: Pepin the Short introduced the Roman Mass into his territory as a means of bringing unity. Imperial ambition and Roman centralization collaborated in this endeavor throughout the Middle Ages. But by the sixteenth century many variations and often superstitious devotions occurred in the Mass. An energetic reform was mandated by Pope Pius V in 1570. However, certain prescribed rites (such as the rite of Lyon, a near relation to that of Rome) were spared this necessary realignment because of their great age and were abandoned only after the Second Vatican Council.

The Roman Mass developed beginning in the fourth century. It followed the example of the African Church, which was the first to adopt the language of the people, that is, Latin. First the congregation (the *Ecclesia*) gathered around the bishop in a *statio;* they then entered in procession with the gospel book, at least from the beginning of the seventh century, and the bishop turned to salute the people: "The Lord be with you!" This movement was accompanied with an entrance hymn, which ended with the *Kyrie eleison* (borrowed from the East and kept in Greek) and the *Gloria in excelsis Deo*—"Glory to God in the highest." Following that, the presider (normally the pope, the bishop of Rome, but in his absence a priest) invited the congregation to pray: *Oremus*—"Let us pray," and in the name of all pronounced a supplication addressed to God the Father.

Many practices were introduced or regularized later, during the Middle Ages and later. Among these were:

Preparation prayers, such as the Confiteor. Various expressions of this particular prayer existed, such as the spare Dominican version: "I confess to God almighty, to the blessed Virgin

Mary, to our Father St. Dominic, to all the saints and to you my brothers, that I have sinned in thought and word, by action and omission, through my own fault; I ask you to pray for me."

Introduction to the sermon. In place of the universal prayer, which disappeared long ago, as the celebrant moved to the pulpit to preach, he invited the congregation to pray: "We pray for peace, the unity of the Church, an increase of faith, the conversion of those who do not know Christ, of heretics, and of schismatics, for the shepherds of the Church (the pope and the local bishop), the king and rulers, the patrons, widows, orphans, the sick, prisoners, women expecting children, travelers, our parents, our friends, etc." This was a long list which ends with "For all our intentions: Our Father . . . Hail Mary . . . I believe in God (a shortened form of the Apostles Creed)." There followed a recitation of the ten commandments of God and the six commandments of the Church. We certainly receive here a full presentation of the Church!

The recitation of the "I believe in God" (chanted at a solemn liturgy, the "High Mass"), according to the longer formula of the Nicene Creed. This was an Eastern custom, first adopted by Charlemagne, then introduced into Rome in the eleventh century. But in the West it included a clause that was not said in the East according to which the Holy Spirit proceeds not only from the Father but also from the Son: this is the *Filioque,* which the Orthodox do not accept.

The use since the eleventh century of unleavened bread, which was easier to keep and was very thin with a round shape and called the "host" (which means "victim"). Since that period there has been an elevation of the host at the consecration. After the words of institution, the celebrant (who has his back to the people) elevates the host and then the chalice to show them to the people. At this time also began the custom of the faithful receiving Communion no longer in the hand but on the tongue, and they no longer receive from the cup. Thomas Aquinas (*Summa theologica* 3, 80, 12) defended this practice in the thirteenth century: for the sacrament to be effected, it suffices that the priest drink from the cup; given the risks of disrespect, it was not necessary that others receive in this fashion.

We should notice that the faithful are on the way to becoming passive spectators. After the preface, the Eucharistic prayer (called the *canon*, which means ''rule'' because it was always the same) was said in a low voice. Communion was no longer distributed during the celebration, but apart from it, before or after, using hosts reserved for that purpose. A final blessing was instituted. Latin was kept as the official language, although it was no longer understood.

In the sixteenth century, the Lord's Supper, to which, moreover, various devotions had been added, honored the saints as much, if not more than, the Living God, and was no longer experienced as it should be. A reform of the liturgy was initiated here and there, but it scarcely began in earnest when the Protestant Reformers intervened.

The Reformers called into question Christ's mode of presence in the Eucharist. Zwingli and Calvin were more radical than Luther, which explains, perhaps, their simplification (when not to say their suppression) of the Eucharistic prayer.

After 1523 with the *Formula Missae*, and 1525 with the *Deutsche Messe*, the latter was reduced in practice by Luther to the institution narrative.

In 1525 Zwingli designed a service of the cenacle; up to the *Sanctus*, there is little change. However, after that he retains only the Our Father, the institution narrative, and the distribution of Communion; and one takes Communion sitting down. Calvin in turn developed his own service at Geneva in 1542 and Knox in Scotland in 1556.

The Reformation also gave birth to the Anglican Church, whose liturgy altered the customary sequence of the celebration but retained a prayer, more one of supplication than of praise, to frame the institution narrative.

In short, with certain modifications, the Liturgy of the Word was preserved by the Reformers, but that of the Eucharist was severely reduced. Moreover, at Geneva the Liturgy of the Word was celebrated every Sunday, but the Eucharist only at Christmas (more exactly, the following Sunday), Easter, Pentecost, and on Reformation Day (to celebrate the beginning of the Reformation by Luther's nailing up his ninety-five theses to the church door on October 31, 1517). Moreover, taking

Communion from the cup was restored. Above all, Latin was abandoned and the local language adopted, which permitted the faithful to participate fully in the celebration.

In 1570, after the Council of Trent which responded to the Protestant crisis, Pope Pius V published a Mass book (a *missal*) which swept away the excessively numerous or luxuriant devotions to the saints and restored to prominence the essentials. Required everywhere, this book provided the foundation for three centuries of liturgical stability. There were only minor modifications in the twentieth century by Pius X and Pius XII before the liturgical reforms of the Second Vatican Council.

The places of Eucharistic celebration in the West are the churches: sometimes humble and sometimes awe-inspiring, their story has been told elsewhere and is well known, moving from pre-Roman down to modern art. Their interiors were embellished with statuary and images, expressions of a living faith and devotions, sometimes authentic and sometimes dubious. Their exteriors varied according to climate and region. In their inspiration and arrangement, however, they remain the heirs and beneficiaries of the basilicas that preceded them.

SUMMARY: *On the topic of the Lord's Supper, the Western tradition appears as a kind of conquest; the Roman liturgy annexed rites which had developed elsewhere (in Spain, France, and Milan) and finally ended by supplanting them altogether. This evolution also witnessed the introduction of extraneous devotions, some of them bordering on superstitions, into the central pascal mystery. This reached the point that, pricked by criticism coming from the Protestant Reform, a serious housecleaning became necessary, which Pope Pius V carried out. The development of liturgical studies in the twentieth century, preparing for and in tandem with the efforts made at the Second Vatican Council, brought further changes.*

CHAPTER THREE

The Different Church Practices

THE BYZANTINE DIVINE LITURGY

Today the Orthodox Churches and the Eastern Catholic Churches almost all use the "divine liturgy" of St. John Chrysostom to celebrate the Lord's Supper. What is its pattern? What does this signify?

Before the liturgy proper begins, there is a preparation by the ministers, that is, the priest who will preside and the deacon who will assist him, as well as any possible concelebrants, in front of the doors. An *iconostasis*, that is, a wall on which are depicted the Savior, the Virgin, and several saints, separates the sanctuary from the rest of the church. Through this wall there are three doors. The ministers venerate the icons of the Savior and the Virgin in front of these doors. They then enter the sanctuary where they vest themselves saying prayers corresponding to the vestments they are putting on and carry out a purification ritual by washing their hands. The opening prayer is well known:

> O Celestial King, Consoler, Spirit of Truth, You who are present everywhere and who fill all, tresure of goods and giver of life, come and remain with us, purify us of all stain, and save our souls, you who are goodness itself.

There follows the preparation of the bread and wine accompanied by specific words and actions. Here the loaves are of leavened bread and rather thick; a first loaf symbolizes the

Lamb, a second is dedicated to the Virgin, and a third to John the Baptist. Pieces are taken from each indicating the apostles, the holy doctors and martyrs, and all the saints. Then the bread and wine is covered with cloths while it is incensed several times, before the altar itself is also incensed. During this period, the congregation chants the office.

The synaxis of the catechumens has six parts:

After an opening blessing there are prayers. They are made before the doors and said by the deacon who invites the people to join with him: "Ever and again let us pray to the Lord in peace." Certain ones are chanted, such as the one invoking the Virgin, which is repeated twice in the course of the ceremony: "Remembering our all holy, immaculate and glorious Lady, the Mother of God and ever virgin Mary, and all the saints, we ourselves offer you, one and all, our entire life to Christ our God." Others are said in a low voice, such as: "Lord, save your people and bless your inheritance. . . ." The congregation joins themselves to this in responding: "Amen; To you, Lord; have mercy."

Next is the "Small Procession." Here the gospel book is carried solemnly, surrounded by candles, with an accompanying song: "Come let us worship and bow down before Christ. Save us, Son of God. Risen from the dead, we sing to you. Alleluia."

Next come the Tropaires, hymns that vary according to the season of the year and the tone of the feast.

There follows the *Trisagion*: "Holy God, Great Holiness, Immortal Holiness," mentioned in the preceding chapter where we discussed the Eastern tradition.

Then come the readings. They are preceded by an invocation to "He who is blessed on the throne of glory" and an introduction. The deacon calls the congregation to attention: "O Wisdom! Let us be alert!" A lector reads the epistle (a passage from a letter from one of the apostles). The Alleluia is sung, during which the deacon incenses the altar, the prepared bread and wine, the sanctuary, the iconostasis, and the congregation. When this is completed, the deacon asks for a blessing and, surrounded by candles, goes to proclaim the Gospel. The assembly echoes his chant: "Glory to you, Lord, glory to you."

The "Prayer for the universal Church" concludes this synaxis. It has two parts: first there are prayer intentions for all the faithful; then an invitation to pray for the catechumens:

> O ye faithful, let us pray for the catechumens, that the Lord may have mercy on them, instruct them in the word of truth, reveal to them the gospel of justice, and unite them to the holy Catholic (that is, universal) and Apostolic Church. Save them, have mercy upon them, help them, keep them, God, through your grace.

The deacon then sends them out: "Catechumens, depart; catechumens, depart, catechumens depart; away with the catechumens."

The Eucharistic synaxis forms a whole that can be divided into eight parts:

Two prayers are said in a low voice by the priest for the intentions of the congregation. They are punctuated with an invocation said in a loud voice, of which this is the first: "To You all glory, honor, and adoration, now and always, forever and ever."

The "Great Procession" is the solemn entrance by which the gifts are brought to the altar. It is at this time that the song of the cherubin is sung:

> Mystically we stand for the cherubin, we sing a song three times holy to the Trinity which gives life, we lay down all care about the world, to receive instead the King of all things, escorted invisibly with an army of angels. Alleluia, Alleluia, Allelulia.

The bread and wine are first incensed, then carried in procession surrounded with candles, during which a prayer for the Church hierarchy and the civil authorities is sung. During all this time, the priest has been saying long prayers in a low voice:

> While in the tomb with your body, in hell with your divine soul, in paradise with the good thief, at the same time you were seated on your throne with the Father and the Holy Spirit, filling everything, Infinite, the Source of Life, truly more precious than paradise and more resplendent than any royal abode; thus appears to us, Christ, your tomb, the source of our resurrection.

A bit later the deacon says: "The Holy Spirit himself will celebrate with us all the days of our life."

At the offering, there are litanies recited by the deacon ("For the precious gifts which have been offered. . . .") and a prayer said in a low voice by the priest.

The ministers then exchange a kiss of peace, kissing each other first on the left shoulder and then on the right, saying: "Christ is in our midst—he is here and will remain here," or, from Easter to the ascension: "Christ is risen—he is truly risen."

Then there is the recitation of the Nicene Creed. The priest next shakes the veil over the bread and wine.

Above we mentioned the Eucharistic prayer, or anaphora, as it is called in the Eastern tradition. It is said in a low voice, except for the "Holy" pronounced three times (cf. Isa 6:3), the words (not the entire account) of institution, the invocation "We offer you what is yours from what is already yours" (that is, "these things which have come from you"), the song of Mary "More venerable than the cherubim and incomparably more glorious than the seraphim," and the remembrance of the living: "recall those whom each one of us carries in our heart . . .," as well as the conclusion which praises the three persons of the Trinity. Several pages from this anaphora are presented in the appendices.

Communion is preceded by a preparation: first petitions; then the Our Father; then a proclamation ("Holy Things for Holy People. Only One is Holy, only One is Lord, Jesus Christ, for the glory of God the Father. Amen"), the breaking of the bread, and the rite of *zéon* already mentioned. Among the prayers which the priest reads at this time is this: "Allow me to share, O Son of God, in your mystical banquet this day, for I will not betray your mysteries to your enemies, and I will not give the kiss of Judas, but rather with the good thief I will proclaim: 'Remember me, Lord, when you come into your Kingdom.' "

There is a Communion song "Receive the body of Christ, drink from the everlasting Spring. . . ." Those wishing to take Communion come forward with their hands crossed over their chests and receive Communion standing; they give their baptismal name and receive on the tongue a cube of Eucharistic bread that has been dipped in the chalice, while the priest says: "The servant of God (he pronounces the name) receives the precious and most holy Body and Blood of our Lord, God, and Savior Jesus Christ, for the remission of their sins and everlasting life." The communicants then step back to pray, after having kissed the base of the chalice. There follow prayers of thanksgiving.

The divine liturgy concludes with a ritual involving a blessing and the distribution of blessed bread. Whatever Eucharistic bread is left over is dipped into the chalice and preserved for the Communion of the sick, but is not made an object of any devotion. It should also be noted that during seasons of penance and on fast days, the divine liturgy is not celebrated.

Such is "the order of the holy and divine liturgy as it is celebrated in the great Church (*Hagia Sophia* in Constantinople) and on the holy mountain (at the monastery on Mount Athos in Greece)." But this sketch of the ceremonial can only hint at the richness of the full experience; one must be present and be immersed within it, be seduced and impregnated with the substance of its rituals and its symbols, with the rhythm of its songs, its words, and its actions. Thus, for example, the preparation of the bread and wine where pieces of bread are pulled off in honor of the Virgin Mary, of John the Baptist, of the great figures of the Old Testament, of the apostles and the saints, symbolize the expectation of the Messiah. The "Small Procession" is the symbol for the entrance of Christ into the world, the "Great Procession" is that of his entrance into his Kingdom and of his Return in glory. The shaking of the veil over the bread and wine recalls the trembling of the angels around the altar. The Eucharistic synaxis represents the death, burial, and resurrection of Christ, his ascension and his reign. The entire divine liturgy is nothing else than the actualization on earth of the celestial liturgy envisioned by the Apostle John on the island of Patmos: "A throne was set up in heaven. . . . Holy, holy is the Lord, the all-powerful God, He who is, who was, and who is to come. . . . You are worthy, Lord our God, to receive glory and power, for You have created all things" (Rev 4; see also chs. 7, 21).

To celebrate the heavenly feast on earth, the faithful are transported for a few hours outside of time. They give expression to the connection that links humankind to God, to whom we aspire and who in turn inclines himself toward us? As a matter of course the faithful prepare themselves for this by fasting and a confession of sins: one must be pure to come close to the Holy. This preparation of hearts occurs before the beginning of the divine liturgy where the priest grooves the bread, indicating thereby the sacrifice of the "Lamb led to the slaughter" (Isa 53:7) and called to become the victorious Lamb of the eternal wedding. The liturgy of the catechumens also carries out a vital assimilation, specifically that of the Word in which one communicates to God through the power of the Spirit. The Eucharistic liturgy, thoroughly filled with the presence of the Spirit invoked to "make of this bread the precious body of Christ and of this chalice the blood of Christ," reaches a climax at the moment of Communion: the universe is then taken on, the Church is gathered, and the believer receives the Eucharist.

This thrusting of humankind, of the Church, and of the world into the time to come takes place in the present: Jesus today transforms and saves, as the words of the priest's blessing and the choral response of the congregation after Communion express:

> Lord, save your people and bless your inheritance.—We have seen the true light, we have received the celestial Spirit, we have found the true faith in adoring the undivided Trinity; for it is the Trinity which has saved us.

SUMMARY: *The divine liturgy of St. John Chrysostom, faithful to the Lord's Supper following the Eastern tradition, includes a preparation, a synaxis of the Word or liturgy of the catechumens, and a synaxis of the Eucharist or liturgy of the faithful. The symbolic words and actions, often reappearing or repeated three times, draw us from earth to heaven: to those who know how to read, to interpret, and to assimilate them, they open a path to prayer, to contemplation, and to reception of the Eucharist. They are at one and the same time catechesis and celebration of the divine mystery.*

THE ROMAN CATHOLIC EUCHARIST

Before the Second Vatical Council some Catholics still believed that they had "satisfied their Sunday obligation" if they arrived at Mass before the liturgy of the Eucharist, during the Offertory prayers, and if they stayed until after the priest's Communion, thereby missing the entire liturgy of the Word, which was sometimes even referred to as the "pre-Mass." However, over the past forty years there has developed a "liturgical movement" intending to restore the meaning of the gathering and to reemphasize the "Twin Tables" of the Word and the Eucharist. This movement exercised an influence over the conciliar reforms; reciprocally, the latter brought this movement to fruition, when the decision of the Constitution on the Liturgy to restore the liturgy and to reform the ritual of the Mass was promulgated on December 4, 1963.

The missal of 1570, with a few modifications, had been continually in use and presented a very servicable scheme of the Mass. We asked God to forgive our sins through the recitation of the *Confiteor* ("I confess to God. . . ."). We sung God praise through the "Gloria" ("Glory to God in the highest. . . .). We requested God's graces through a prayer the priest said called the "Collect." God spoke to us through the two readings from holy Scripture (one was always from the Gospels), and through the preaching. We offered God the bread and wine (with our lives "in a spirit of humility and with a contrite heart") so that they might be consecrated and returned to us as food. However, the use of Latin and the often rapid recitition of the prayers, without any commentary or explanation, despite many efforts to remedy the situation by clarifications in catechism classes and by vernacular translations (at least more recently), hardly permitted the faithful to truly participate—all the more so because many came only to satisfy their Sunday obligation. For this reason the missal of

Paul VI, after the Council, planned for a stronger participation by the faithful.

In a short time the use of Latin was abandoned (although the official texts to which all translations and adaptations must refer themselves are still written in Latin).

The status of hymns called "propers," that is to say, those which vary according to the Sunday or the feast and are intended to be sung at the entrance, between the two readings, at the offertory, and at Communion, has not been reduced. Instead, however, of being performed by a choir called the *schola*, they are usually sung by the congregation, at least in their refrains.

The entrance ritual no longer includes the "prayers at the foot of the altar" (Ps 43 "Do me justice, O Lord, and plead my cause," and the *Confiteor*), but rather a greeting like "The grace of Our Lord Jesus Christ, the love of God the Father, and the fellowship of the Holy Spirit be with you always" (cf. 2 Cor 13:14). Also there is a choice of penitential formulas, of which the "I confess to God. . . ." is only one.

The selection of readings provides a greater variety of biblical texts, especially from the New Testament. Further, the profession of faith, the "I believe in God . . .," may include the Apostles Creed as well as the Nicene Creed.

The universal prayer is restored as it was in the time of Pope Gelasius.

The offertory has been especially modified. Whereas before the bread and wine were "offered" while ephasizing their unworthiness, now there is a "preparation of the gifts" that thanks God for the fruits of the earth and the vine, called to become the bread of life and the wine of the everlasting Kingdom, as they are in the Jewish liturgy.

Formerly there was only one Eucharistic prayer together with at most a dozen possible prefaces; the prayer remains, shorn of some high-flown and melodramatic phrases, and may now be joined with one of more than twenty-four prefaces. Above all, the new missal has been enriched with several alternate Eucharistic prayers. All are said in a loud voice that may be heard by the people, and all priests present are urged to concelebrate.

The Communion rituals are the same: the "Our Father," the kiss of peace, the fraction rite, the "Lamb of God," but now accompanied with less florid prayers; and the exchange of peace is extended by the priest to all the faithful. Above all one now takes Communion standing, whereas before one knelt at the Communion rail, considered as the limit of the sanctuary. Also, one receives Communion "under both species," that is, from the cup as well, and receives the host in the hand as was the ancient custom: "As you approach . . . , form your left hand into a throne for your right hand, for the latter is to receive the King, and in the crux of your hand receive the Body of Christ, saying: Amen" (Cyril of Jerusalem, Mystagogical Catechesis V, 27). The celebration no longer concludes with the *Ite, missa est*—"Go, It is finished," but rather with "Go in the peace of Christ" as in the East.

Without doubt the most original new Eucharistic prayer is that known as the Third, created to bring about an alternative to the one Eucharistic prayer in use before the council and now referred to as the First Eucharistic Prayer. Deriving both its form and many of its formulas from ancient Eucharistic prayers, it nevertheless is not modeled strictly on any one of them and goes to some length to respond to contemporary pastoral needs.

There is no specified preface before the *Sanctus;* therefore, one can use any preface with it. Of course, we should stress that the preface is an integral part of the Eucharistic prayer; but after the *Sanctus*, this prayer seems to contain another preface:

> Father, you are holy indeed, and all creation rightly gives you praise. All life, all holiness comes from you through your Son, Jesus Christ our Lord, by the working of the Holy Spirit. From age to age you gather a people to yourself, so that from east to west a perfect offering may be made to the glory of your name.

This is theme of salvation history.

It continues thus: "And so, Father, we bring you these gifts. We ask you to make them holy by the power of your Spirit, that they may become the body and blood of your Son, our

Lord Jesus Christ, at whose command we celebrate this eucharist." God is asked to consecrate the bread and wine through his Spirit; this is a consecrating epiclesis:

> On the night he was betrayed, he took bread and gave you thanks and praise. He broke the bread, gave it to his disciples, and said: "Take this, all of you, and eat it: this is my body which will be given up for you." When supper was ended, he took the cup. Again he gave you thanks and praise, gave the cup to his disciples, and said: "Take this, all of you, and drink from it: this is the cup of my blood, the blood of the new and everlasting covenant. It will be shed for you and for all, so that sins may be forgiven. Do this in memory of me."

This is the institution narrative.

The congregation then acclaims the "mystery of the faith": the death, the resurrection, and the return in glory of the Savior.

Then comes a "memorial" which is simultaneously a prayer of offering and of thanksgiving: it should be appreciated as the expression of our recognition of the unique gift that God has given us in Jesus Christ:

> Father, calling to mind the death your Son endured for our salvation, his glorious resurrection and ascension into heaven, and ready to greet him when he comes again, we offer you in thanksgiving this holy and living sacrifice.

Here is the anamnesis:

> Look with favor on your Church's offering, and see the Victim whose death has reconciled us to yourself. Grant that we, who are nourished by his body and blood, may be filled with his Holy Spirit, and become one body, one spirit in Christ. May he make us an everlasting gift to you. . . .

This prayer merits two remarks. The word "offering," which one could also translate "sacrifice," is the most appropriate for indicating the precise connection between our Eucharist which makes present the meal Jesus conducted on the eve of his death and his sacrifice on the Cross. Secondly, this request made to the Holy Spirit to bring about the unity of Christians does not simply repeat the consecrating epiclesis that preceded the institution narrative. The earlier was said over the gifts, the later is over the congregation. Moreover, it is at this moment that Hippolytus of Rome placed his *epiclesis:*

> We beg you to send your Holy Spirit over the offering of the Holy Church. May all those you have gathered here together share in the holy mysteries and be filled with the Holy Spirit. . . . (THE APOSTOLIC TRADITION 4).

A good number of ancient anaphoras locate here a formula of consecrating epiclesis, thereby indicating that it is God who consecrates through the Holy Spirit. However, the Catholic Church regulates the ritual in the matter of the sacraments; in her eyes, it is the words pronounced by Jesus in the institution narrative that are "the words of consecration," and their omission would invalidate the sacrament. However, the Alexandrian tradition and that of France, as well as the Mosarabic liturgy, all have an epiclesis over the gifts *before* the institution narrative. As a compromise, the Third Eucharistic Prayer contains a consecrating *epiclesis* over the gifts, and a Communion epiclesis over the congregation.

It continues with intercessory prayers for our salvation, for the world, and for the Church. The virgin Mary is there described as the "holy Mother of God." The virgin is said to be "holy" because the Catholic faith believes that those who have been saved continue to share in the communion of saints at the end of their human existence. She is called the Mother of God because her son is "true God and true man," because "she gave birth to the Word of God made flesh according to the flesh," as Cyril of Alexandria writes in a letter addressed to Nestorius, patriarch of Constantinople, a formula quoted by the Council of Ephesus in 431 (at a time when the distinct Churches were still united). From there, the prayer spreads out to include all the members of the Body of Christ: the saints in heaven, the living and the dead, to end with the glory of the Father shared by the Son in the unity of the Spirit. Let us quote this intercession so that the reader may have a complete experience of this Eucharistic prayer:

May the Holy Spirit make us an everlasting gift to you and enable us to share in the inheritance of your saints, with Mary, the virgin mother of God; with the apostles, the martyrs, St. . . . [one mentions the saint whose feast it is or the patron of that church] and all your saints, on whose constant intercession we rely for help. Lord, may this sacrifice, which has made our peace with you, advance the peace and salvation of all the world. Strengthen in faith and love your pilgrim Church on earth; your servant Pope . . . , our bishop . . . (one names them), and all the bishops, with the clergy and the entire people your son has gained for you. Father, hear the prayers of the family you have gathered here before you. In mercy and love unite all your children wherever they may be. Welcome into your kingdom our departed brothers and sisters, and all who have left this world in your friendship. We hope to enjoy for ever the vision of your glory, through Christ our Lord, from whom all good things come. Through him, with him, in him, in the unity of the Holy Spirit, all glory and honor is yours, almighty Father, for ever and ever. Amen.

The missal of Paul VI currently in use also includes two other Eucharistic prayers: the second, inspired by the tradition of Hippolytus, and the fourth, inspired by the anaphora of St. Basil. These are included in the appendices.

Several national missals have also developed Eucharistic prayers described variously as "for reconciliation," "for large congregations," or "for children," all approved by the Roman authorities.

We see, therefore, that in conformity with the liturgical traditions, the conciliar reform has succeeded in unifying the diverse styles, all the while avoiding uniformity. As the Gospel message spreads to the entire world, will this diversity be sufficient? Ethnic groups have askesd to celebrate according to their own rituals. For example, a Zairean rite has just been approved by Rome; it succeeds in being both faithful to the tradition and open to the sensitivities of the people.

Within this rite the traditional structure has continued, except that the penitential preparation has been displaced until after the Liturgy of the Word, so that the experience of repentance grows out of hearing the Word of God. The petitions for forgiveness may be quoted: "As an insect attaches itself to the skin and sucks the blood of a person, so evil has infested us . . . ." Such daily experiences from the life of the people have been integrated within the liturgy. Here are two entrance rites. The community gather like a clan around its chief whom they salute in the traditional fashion with the *losako* ("Good Day"). The ancestors are invoked: the dancers bend down to beg them to grant success to their performance. Is there a risk of syncretism here? We must remember: "Is God only the god of the Jews? Is he not also the god of the pagans?" (Rom 3:29; see also 2:14-17). A sense of choreography is also present; the entrance procession is accompanied by the sound of instruments and to the rhythm of drums, the crowd in loin cloths and the ministers dressed with the *boubous* with bright colors; the offertory procession takes place as a dance. If this kind of dancing were not allowed in the liturgy, the local population would be lost to the sects.

The canon derives from the Second Eucharistic Prayer shorn of various acclamations and enriched by various emendations, such as: "Through him you have created all things, you have created the heavens and the earth, our river the Zaire, our streams and lakes, the animals that dwell in our forests, and the fish which swim in our waters; the things that we see and the things that we do not see."

As exotic as such adaptations may seem, they are indispensable; people of an oral civilization need to see, mime, dance, chat about, and create if they are to properly express themselves; a written text that is passed on, even if it is properly translated and well presented, remains foreign to their mental categories. Because she did not understand the necessity of similar transformations during the seventeenth century, Rome contributed to the failure of the China mission that had been so well initiated by various missionaries. May her efforts find more success this time!

SUMMARY: *In the Catholic Church where the liturgy has remained stable since the Counter-Reformation that followed the Council of Trent, one must be a fervent and well instructed Christian to participate truly in the Eucharistic mystery. Building upon a liturgical move-*

ment that is still in progress, the liturgical reform inaugurated by the Second Vatican Council hopes to facilitate just this kind of participation: the abandonment of Latin, instruction in the mystery at the very heart of the celebration, new Eucharistic prayers inspired by the ancient ones and responding to contemporary needs, etc.— elements all rooted in a tradition of creative fidelity!

THE PROTESTANT LORD'S SUPPER

Until the most recent reforms in the liturgy, some Catholics had fallen into the habit of arriving a bit late for Mass; for to "assist at Mass" it was not necessary to be present for the Liturgy of the Word, where various passages were read in Latin and were hardly comprehensible to the people. In the same way, but in the opposite direction, some Protestants, while faithful to their Sunday worship—taken up entirely with prayer and proclamation—felt no obligation to stay for the Lord's Supper which followed. As a consequence, the latter was celebrated only about once a month, and the departure of a substantial portion of the congregation who elected not to participate was even anticipated by the liturgy. Later the Lord's Supper, or cenacle (from the Latin *cena,* or light meal, a name used since the early days of the Reformation), began to be integrated within the normal worship service. What was the transition from the Roman Mass to the Protestant *Lord's Supper,* and how is the latter celebrated today?

The early Reformers had no intention of setting up a new Church, but rather of reforming the one Church. In what concerns the Eucharistic celebration, they proposed to restore the Liturgy of the Word, to render it intelligible and accessible to all, and to ensure that the celebration would be at the same time an instruction that could nourish the faith. This happened, in fact, very rapidly at Strasbourg; it took only fifteen years to pass from the Mass to the Lord's Supper.

There from February 16, 1524, the priest Diebold Schwartz began celebrating the Mass in German with the adaptations mentioned above. The basic structure and elements were retained, but already the prayers were changed from the singular to the plural, indicating that all were celebrating, and not the priest alone. Above all, the offertory was changed; the Mass was no longer understood as a sacrifice, but as an offering where what is offered is not bread and wine, but the faithful themselves. "I therefore exhort you, brothers, to offer yourselves as a living sacrifice, holy and agreeable to God; this will be your spiritual worship" (Rom 12:1). There was no preaching and no singing.

At the end of the year this liturgy changed more through the influence of ex-Dominican Martin Kuhorn, also called Bucer, with borrowings from some German liturgies already in use: the Apostles' Creed as an option, a choice of prefaces—which soon disappeared entirely—the removal of special liturgies for feasts, an optional blessing according to the Aaronic formula: "May the Lord turn his face upon you and give you peace" (Num 6:24-26), the use of red wine the color of blood, an invocation of the Trinity after the Communion, and the canticle of Simeon (Luke 2:29-32).

The next year the words "the Lord's Supper" (*Herren Nachtmal*) and "Mass," "pastor" (*Pfarrherr*) and "priest," were placed next to each other in the books, but now everything was translated into German; the Apostles Creed appeared first, before the Nicene Creed, and various actions, such as the elevation of the host and the cup, were eliminated. The many blessings and signs of the cross, and the practice of mixing water with wine in the cup were omitted. The sermon appeared together with singing by the congregation. Further, the service ended with Luther's hymn "Praise God through whom all. . . ."

More changes followed: the pastor was called the "server" (*Diener*); he now turned to face the people and explained the scriptural texts he had chosen. A table replaced the altar. The Apostles' Creed replaced the Nicene Creed. The institution narrative was reduced to the account in 1 Corinthians 11, without any embellishments from outside the text.

Between 1526 and 1537 the *Kyrie* and the *Gloria* disappeared and were replaced with a psalm; similarly, the preface and the *Sanctus* vanished, replaced with a prayer of thanksgiving. The blessing "in the name of the Father, of the Son, and of the Holy Spirit" gave way to the non-Trinitarian Aaronic formula (cf. Num 6:24-26). Special liturgical vestments were no longer employed. Singing by the congregation and the server's sermon assumed a larger place. There was no longer a daily celebration, but only once a week in the cathedral, and more rarely still in other churches.

Without being ordained a priest, John Calvin celebrated a primitive Mass near Poitier in 1534, which was reduced to the institution narrative and the distribution of bread and wine. In 1536 in Geneva he witnessed the first liturgy in French presented by Farel. In Strasbourg in 1539 he witnessed the German worship service, and it inspired his own liturgy, which appeared at Geneva in 1542.

From this point on, celebrations of the Lord's Supper evolved and diversified rapidly: Luther's Mass in Germany, the cenacle of Zwingli in Zurich, Cramner's Prayer Book in England, that of John Knox in Scotland, and that of John Calvin for Geneva and the kingdom of France. They all more or less derived from the Roman Mass stripped of its excess foliage and enriched with new elements, and they continued to evolve, in both good and bad ways. For the better through the work of those continuing the work of Calvin were people like Ostervald in the eighteenth century at Neuchatel, Bersier in the nineteenth in Paris (the founder of the Star Temple), and Paquier in the twentieth century in the Canton of Vaud. They were all attentive to the spiritual needs of their flocks and made great efforts to remain faithful to the spirit of John Calvin and to penetrate to very sources of the liturgical traditions in the primitive Church. For the worse, there were later developments influenced, not always positively, by new theological doctrines and philosophical ideas. A happier influence was the ecumenical work carried out through the "Liturgy of the Reformed Church of France," which appeared for the first time in 1950 and was approved by the National Council in 1962, in which the Lord's Supper is firmly integrated within the worship service.

This liturgy had four parts (preparation, the Word, the Holy Supper, and a missioning or sending forth) with the option

of omitting the Holy Supper, since it is not celebrated every
Sunday.

The first part began with a welcome using the language of
the Bible: "Grace and peace be given to you by God our Father and Jesus Christ our Savior" (Titus 1:4) or a liturgical formula: "The Lord be with you," followed by an invocation
where the congregation sings the canticle "Lord, be in our
midst" and words of adoration such as "O eternal One, you
are God, and there is no other god but you" (Deut 4:35), followed by a hymn. Then the proclamation of the Law of God
followed: ten variations were proposed in view of the Ten
Commandments of God (cf. Exod 20:3-17) or that of Jesus (the
love of God and of one's neighbor; cf. Matt 22:37-39) up to
the counsels of harmony and humility (cf. Phil 2:2-7), while
also employing the Gospels and Paul's letters. There followed
a confession of sins, with an ample choice among biblical texts
(Ps 51 for example) or of diverse inspiration such as the *Venite
adoremus* of the Roman liturgy; a proclamation of pardon: "God
grants you pardon for your sins," also included numerous biblical variations. Next the congregation was invited to give
thanks through a canticle before the Profession of Faith: the
Apostles' Creed or that of Nicea, or perhaps another profession from the Reform tradition. Instructions were printed as
to when to sit, stand up, kneel down, or bow.

Is this first part in conformity with the Reform tradition? The
Ten Commandments appeared in Geneva for the first time only
in 1639 and were placed before the confession of sins as if to
call the congregation to repentence; this order was retained
as a traditional element. Earlier, however, Calvin, the shep-
herd to the French immigrants in Strasbourg, had announced
them *after* the confession of sins, as if to invite the repentent
sinners to live according to the law; this was the meaning of
his invitation to listen to the law: "Listen, brothers, how God
wishes to be served."

The second part opened with a "Prayer for Illumination"
with eight possible variations, and said while bowing or kneel-
ing down "to ask God for understanding concerning his
Word." For through the reading from the Bible extended in
a canticle or a psalm, and through the preaching that followed,

also punctuated by a hymn, it was indeed God who spoke to his people. There followed announcements and the offering accompanied by an appropriate text such as "There is greater happiness in giving than in receiving" (Act 20:35). Finally, this part concluded with an intercessory prayer (a choice of three), that is to say, a universal prayer, which ends with the Our Father. For if the Lord's Supper was not to be celebrated, this was in effect the end of the worship. After that there was only an exhortation addressed to the congregation while it remained standing (for example, the proclamation of the beatitudes from Matt 5:3-10), and a blessing which the presider pronounced with his hands extended over the people to dismiss them in peace. Any member of the congregation could have spoken after the homily to give thanks and at the time of intercessions to mention a special intention.

So far everything was as expected; for is not the Word the essential part, the skeleton, and the center of Protestant worship? It does not consist of a discourse about God, but of a Word from God (every preacher should be imbued with it!); that is why the reading opened with this invitation: "Listen, brothers, to the Word of God," and the preaching ended with a period of meditation in silence or supported by soft music from the organ as a background.

Here was the order of the Lord's Supper: it began with a preface, with a choice of three inspired by Eastern anaphoras, all of which led to the *Sanctus.* Then came an institution narrative taken either from 1 Corinthians 11:23-26 or from Matthew 26:20, 26-29. There followed a Prayer of the the Lord's Supper which could be called a Eucharistic prayer, for it includes an anamnesis and an epiclesis. There was a choice of two.

The first reads:

> Holy and just Father, as we commemorate here the unique and perfect sacrifice offered once for all on the cross by our Lord Jesus Christ, in the joy of his resurrection and awaiting his coming, we offer ourselves to you as a living and holy sacrifice.

This is an *anamnesis.*
Further on one reads:

> Send your Holy Spirit over us so that, in taking from this bread
> and this cup, it be given to us to share in the body and blood
> of our Lord Jesus Christ. For it is through him that you create,
> you sanctify, you give life, you bless, and that you give us all
> good things.

This is an *epiclesis*.

After the anamnesis there was a prayer for purification: "You
who know hearts, purify and renew your forgiveness in us.
Make us live through the life of the Risen One; may he remain
in us and we in him." After the epiclesis, a short quotation
from the *Didaché* followed. There was a slight pause between
each of these four elements.

Here is the second optional prayer:

> Recalling, O holy and just Father, the life and work of your be-
> loved Son, of his passion and death, of his resurrection and of
> his ascension, we await the day when he will come in his power
> and glory. In this expectation we carry out now the command
> he gave us. Father, behold the bread and wine we have from
> him: we give you thanks for these visible signs of the sacrifice
> that he offered you for us on the cross.—In communion with
> him, our high priest and intercessor, we present to you our-
> selves and all our goods. We ask you to consecrate them to your
> service, as a living and holy offering. Send your Spirit over us
> so that he might sanctify us, renew us, and that, in participa-
> tion in this bread and this wine, we might share in the body
> and blood of your Son. Thereby may all who receive from this
> bread and this cup be united in one sole body, and may we
> grow in Jesus Christ, the head of the Church, who lives and
> reigns with you, in the union of the Holy Spirit, for ever and
> ever. Amen.

This prayer thus included both an anamnesis and an epiclesis.

In both prayers the doctrinal emphases are clear: a com-
memoration of the sacrifice of Christ "unique and perfect,
offered once for all," an invocation of the Holy Spirit over the
people, not over the gifts, a thanksgiving for "this bread and
this wine that we receive from him (Christ), these visible signs
of the sacrifice that he offered for us on the cross," union with
Christ: "so that he may remain in us and we in him." This
was a rich and concise prayer that derived from the earliest

anaphoras, but now pruned of the excessive moralizing amplifications of the liturgies of the succeeding centuries which did not focus on these Eucharistic elements in the same precise way.

The Communion began with a modest invitation to come forward to the table so as to surround it, in successive waves if necessary, one pew at a time. This was the highpoint of the Lord's Supper, with the breaking of the bread: "The bread which we break, is it not a sharing in the body of Our Lord Jesus Christ, who was broken for us"—"This cup of blessing for which we give thanks, is it not a sharing in the blood of Our Lord Jesus Christ, the blood of the new covenant which was poured out for us" (cf. 1 Cor 10:16). After each pew came forward, the communicants returned to their places with a word of peace. Then the congregation was invited to give voice to its praise, for example, with Psalm 103 "O bless the Lord, my soul . . . ."

The formula of the fraction rite "the cup of blessing for which we give thanks" was not exactly that of our Bibles, which have instead the "cup of blessing which we bless." The latter have translated the Greek word *eúlogoûmen* as "we bless," to remain faithful to the Jewish liturgy. But this word also signifies "we praise, we give thanks," and such a translation fits better with the Eucharistic praise.

The fourth part of the Reform liturgy consisted in an exhortation and a blessing, as was indicated above appropriate to the worship service without a Lord's Supper.

This "Liturgy of the French Reformed Church," published in 1963, achieved a cultural and Eucharistic unity for this Church and also influenced certain other denominations.

Apparently, at least since 1802, after the ending of the persecutions which the French Protestants had endured earlier, the French Reformed Churches followed for the most part the practices of Geneva. Several observations, nonscientific but telling, give some idea of the changes that have occurred.

Since the attempts in 1724 and 1743 to revise the "Ecclesiastical Prayers" received from Calvin, none of the liturgies adopted in succession (1861, 1875, 1897) included an anamnesis or epiclesis until 1945. The liturgy of 1897 still contained the words of excommunication: "We declare unworthy to participate in this holy sacrament the impious, the unbelieving, any obstinate sinners, and all those who live irregular lives." It still affirms that the Lord's Supper retains "all that is most holy and most consoling in the Christian faith" (was this Calvin's doctrine maintaining that Jesus therein makes us sharers in his body and blood?) (*Christian Institutions* IV, XVII, 1–32). A call is made for an examination of conscience. Of course, the prayer of the Lord's Supper touches on the theme of the history of Salvation, but there is no liturgical preface culminating in a *Sanctus*. On the other hand, the words of the fraction rite, "the bread which we break . . . the cup of blessing that we bless. . . ." (cf. 1 Cor 10:16) which are to be found as one option among others in the liturgy of 1743, have become firmly anchored in the Reform tradition. In a way, they ratify the action of the Holy Spirit in the sacrament. It was still that way in the liturgy of 1897.

However, the liturgy of 1963 unifies the Reform tradition and that of the ancient and undivided Church. In this action there is a convergence with the liturgical reforms undertaken by the Catholic Church since the Second Vatican Council. From now on these two liturgies place our Churches on the road to a common Eucharistic faith.

The liturgy of the evangelical Lutheran Churches is also in conformity with the ancient tradition. For example, the prayer entitled "Consecration" from their First Liturgy (quoted in an appendix to this book) differs hardly at all from the Second and Third Eucharistic Prayers of the Roman Catholic liturgy.

We might ask, what is the Lord's Supper like in those Churches which derive from the Protestant reformation that describe themselves as "free" or "independent" (federated or not), who prefer to call themselves Evangelical Churches, and who seem to be growing rapidly?

Certain follow existing liturgies with a few liberties, retaining the main elements, or at least being inspired by them. Others develop their own traditions. The majority, it seems, hold themselves to the Word of God, as it is found in the Gospels and the Epistles. This is the justification for the thanksgiving: "Sing your gratitude to God in your hearts with

psalms, hymns, and songs inspired by the Spirit'' (Col 3:16).
''Take, eat . . . Drink from this all of you'' is the justification
for the sharing in the bread and wine which Jesus carried out
and referred to as his body and blood, and the way in which
he should be remembered. This Lord's Supper is thus brief
and simple; it consists in a ''taking, blessing, breaking, and
giving'' carried out in obedience and submission to the Word.

SUMMARY: *The Protestant Lord's Supper was born out of the
Catholic Mass that was in use around the year 1520. By pruning
away the overgrowth and strengthening it with new elements, there
developed a Liturgy of the Word which became the principal act of
worship. The Eucharistic liturgy became a separate action called the
Lord's Supper (principally by suppressing the offertory that served
as the transition to the "sacrificial liturgy"). The French Reformed
Churches adopted the liturgy of John Calvin published in Geneva in
1542 and revised it over the centuries. The most recent revision, carried out by the French Reformed Church and published in 1963, as-
similates the traditions of the Reformed Churches with those of the
ancient and undivided Churches. Since the liturgical reforms of the
Roman Catholic Church and the Lutheran liturgy are orienting themselves toward the same ancient tradition, the mainline Churches are
working toward a common Eucharistic faith. However, with some
exceptions, the independent Evangelical Churches or those attached
to a federation (not to be confused with the Evangelical Lutheran
Churches) hold themselves to the information recorded in the Bible.*

CHAPTER FOUR

Questions About the Lord's Supper

IS THIS THE LORD'S SUPPER?

The Word of God found in the Gospels and the Letters of Paul to the Corinthians reveals to us the precise and ever-relevant connection between the last meal of Jesus and his one sacrifice on the cross. Further, the story of the disciples on the way to Emmaus (cf. Luke 24) teaches us that Christ allows himself to be recognized in the renewal of this meal. The history of the first Christian meals after the time of the Apostles shows us how the latter became the place for the recognition in faith of Jesus now absent but still present after his resurrection. Consequently it is the place for the birth and growth of the Christian faith in the risen Jesus and also the milieu in which the Gospel texts were produced. An overly literal or fundamentalist reading of the institution narratives (which too easily forgets the episode of the disciples on the road to Emmaus) hardly permits us to recognize the Risen One there.

The tradition of the Churches in the following centuries illustrates the importance of this recognition, in that they created the prayers of *anamnesis* and *epiclesis*. ''To recall'' Jesus's Last Supper does not only mean remembering how it went, but also to take into account all that this action symbolized and contained: the cross, the resurrection, and the return in Glory. Further, to profit from the presence of the One who is with us until the end of time (cf. Matt 28) can only from now on come about through the active presence of his Spirit. These thoughts allow us to distinguish whether certain celebrations of the cenacle or of the Eucharist in our time (independently of the faith of the celebrants and participants, which is not in question here) are indeed the Lord's Supper.

A first example might be that of the holy meal celebrated during the meeting of a free Evangelical Church of pentacostal orientation. After a worship service of sufficient duration celebrated with expressive songs of praise, and a healing service where several members of the congregation have come forward for prayers to be said appropriate to their illness and made "in the name of Jesus," the presider, more a leader than a celebrant, announces with simplicity that "now we will begin the holy cenacle."

He then moves to a small table placed to one side (the only table in the room), and removing a white cloth, he uncovers the bread and wine. The wine is poured into small glasses for individual use, the bread is cut into small cubes about a quarter inch on a side. A helper, probably an elder, comes forward at this point, and the distribution begins and continues through the pews. It lasts only a few minutes.

Let us say again that the faith of the members of this congregation is not here in question, whatever it may be—baptized in the Holy Spirit, baptized in water (in this Church or in another), or perhaps not even baptized at all. Even if they have the full intention of obeying the Lord's command "Do this in memory of me," has this congregation truly recreated the "taking, blessing, breaking, and giving" which is the content and meaning of Jesus's words and deeds? As evocative as it may be, has there been here anything more than a friendly action which did not even include the words Jesus is recorded as saying? Is this authentically the Lord's Supper?

Another example, with many more distinctions, and thus with much to teach us, is that of a Eucharist celebrated during a get-together of young people around sixteen years of age in a Catholic chapel. At the end of two full days of enjoyment but also of study and reflection, the youth are invited to understand that they may not "sit down at this table in the same way as they do at a conventional meal," but that first they must recognize each other as friends, companions who have come together to form a group, young men and women who "think well of each other" but who also "have trouble occasionally

in putting up with, in understanding, or in liking one another."
A reading and a song amplify this theme, and the invitation
points them toward the recognition of the Lord: "We must
recognize the presence in our midst of someone who is still
and will remain forever unknown by all," someone who elicits
mocking taunts from our friends if we say we believe in him,
"someone who we are searching for and who we will always
be searching for." At this point a young person reads a prayer.

Then the priests present move behind a table for the Eucharist, whose celebration has three steps: an offering, or more
exactly an expression of the prayer intentions; words over the
bread and wine framed by a prayer developed from liturgical
tradition; and a sharing of the loaf by all.

The prayer intentions are invited, written down, and
presented. They are solicited through an opening prayer,
something like the following:

> O God, we want to talk to You. We know for sure that our
> desires and prayers are all tainted with self-love; but still, take
> us this evening as we are. Sometimes it helps us to express out
> loud the things we want to pray about, for we are all more or
> less the same, and tonight we feel ourselves deeply bonded.
> We do not want to use conventional prayers; who tonight, after
> all, is honestly thinking about children starving in a foreign land?
> Instead, we want to talk about things that really bother us or
> are personal in our lives. For example, I want to get good
> enough grades to pass in school this year; I ask you to help me
> fight less with my brothers; to be less of a pain to my friends;
> that people may understand me better; that I might get along
> better with girls; that so-and-so might not be so hostile to me,
> etc.

Those present then organize their intentions into bunches
which they present separated by a refrain.

The Eucharistic prayer then begins:

> God, we will now divide this loaf. We can do so now because we
> are ready. We may do so because one day a long time ago
> a man said to his friends (one of the priests continues): "Each
> time that you come together as friends, as brothers and sisters,
> if you desire it, I will be with you. And I will help you find out

who you are, and who God is. And I will help you to understand each other better so that you may better love one another.''

The narrative continues:

We can do this because this same Jesus Christ took bread from the table at which he was dining with his friends, prayed with them and said to them [all the priests say together]: ''Take this bread and divide it among yourselves to everyone who wants it. Together eat this bread. It is the sign that I am with you.''

The words over the wine are then spoken:

In the same way at the end of the meal he took a cup of wine from this same table and said to his friends (all the priests continue): ''Drink from this cup. For all time it will be a sign that I am with you.''

The prayer continues:

And since that day all over the world, thousands, even millions of times, millions of people like us, in every country have shared in this same bread, so as to better love one another, to better discover You, Lord, and the love which you bring to us. And tonight we do the same, together with our leader [one mentions the bishop's name and the territory of the diocese] who strives daily to be the friend of all, young or old, who are seeking God. O God, you require from us a great act of trust. You ask us to believe that this bread is not only nourishment for our body, but also the sign that a person still lives with us, a very mysterious person, Jesus, so much so that sometimes we ask ourselves if this person is not simply Yourself, God, who wishes so much to live among us.

The prayer concludes with an exhortation:

We each are going to make this act of trust before You. Each one of us, in silence, and each in his or her own way. Respecting the privacy of our neighbor on both sides, we send forth our most personal prayer, the prayer that we dare not tell even our closest friend, for it is the deepest secret in our lives.

The third stage is the Communion service. To mark its introduction, there is a period of reflection with perhaps some quiet music played on a saxophone in the background, together with a brief song that rises and falls. The Our Father is recited by all, and then the loaf is divided in an informal way, with each one taking what he or she wishes and consuming it immediately. The music and singing conclude before the group reforms to join those who have not participated in this celebration.

There is no doubt about the considerable pedagogic value and powerful success of such a celebration of the Eucharist, which is all the more difficult to bring about in that such a group normally consists of young people who have been baptized but who, because they have not been encouraged to have a personal encounter with the Lord, are still looking, and should be considered more or less as catechumens. As a matter of fact, because of its way of unfolding and its language, this kind of celebration should doubtless be as a means of catechesis. But was this truly the Lord's Supper? Was this really the Eucharist?

For, from the point of view of the Catholic Church, there are too many shortcomings to it for it to live up to a full Eucharist.

During the period preceding the Eucharist, the individual lives of the young people have certainly been touched upon; also an invitation was extended to look for ''some one among us who is now and will forever remain mysterious to us.'' However, there has been no hearing of the Word of God.

As for the offering, prayer intentions have certainly been expressed, but here again, these young people have at most given voice to their personal concerns without integrating them within the overall movement of the people of God, without having had to ''offer themselves as a living sacrifice, holy and acceptable to God, . . . in spiritual worship'' (cf. Rom 12:1).

In the Eucharistic prayer, there was indeed mention of this ''man, Jesus Christ'' who distributed bread and wine, and even of ''a person so mysterious that sometimes we wonder if this person is not simply You, God, who wishes to live among us.'' But is this enough for a conscious, explicit, and true confession of faith in Jesus Christ, Dead and Risen?

Two elements especially are missing: the memorial of Easter and the invocation of the Holy Spirit. The bread and wine are presented as a "sign" of the presence of Jesus, our Friend. Doubtless this is a powerful image for adolescents, but the Lord's Supper, the memorial of Easter, is of an entirely different order: "This is my Body given for you. . . my blood poured out for you. . . ." And doesn't the Holy Spirit have to be mentioned, in fact to address oneself to him to ask him to make of us an offering to the glory of the Father (the Third Catholic Eucharistic Prayer), instead of beginning the prayer by simply announcing: "We can now share this bread because we are ready," when in fact we would never be ready without the help of the Spirit?

Thus the Communion is a part of what precedes it: the bread is distributed, a loaf of friendship. But is Jesus present as the One who serves? Is it his body that is being shared?

We can recognize the catechetical purposes of those who developed this style of liturgy. However, even with the intention of using it as a means of initiation, we are not totally free to manipulate the Eucharist in any way, even for a good purpose, for we are dealing here specifically with something we have received which we have pledged ourselves to carry on in the same manner that it was given to us: "This is what I received from the Lord," writes Paul, "and what I have passed on to you" (1 Cor 11:23). It is the gathering of a community of believers, a renewal of the celebration of Easter, the sacrament of our unity in the faith, the sacrament of the Body of Christ. It connotes a fidelity to the liturgical tradition. Now, tradition does not mean simple repetition, but rather creative fidelity, as the developments already presented in this book have illustrated; the various Churches understand this and demonstrate it when they create new anaphoras rooted in the tradition to respond to emerging needs of the people of God, as in this "Eucharistic Prayer for a Group of young people" developed within the Catholic Church, whose anamnesis and epiclesis run as follows:

> We are gathered here before you, Father. Filled with joy, we recall what Jesus did to save us; in this offering that he bestowed upon the Church, we celebrate his death and resurrection; Father in heaven, accept us with your dearly beloved Son.

Jesus desired to give his life for us. You raised him up, Father; for this we praise you. [Acclamation] "He lives now at your right hand. He is with us for all times and in all places." [Acclamation] "He will come one day in the glory of his Kingdom; then no one will be sad, sick, or unhappy any more." [Acclamation]

"Father, we are going to receive from this table, in the joy of the Holy Spirit, the body and blood of Christ; may this Communion enable us to live as Jesus lived, devoted entirely to You and to our neighbor."

SUMMARY: *Have we attained truly the Lord's Supper when Christians simply give voice to their lived experiences in a ritual which contains conspicuous omissions from what is generally acknowledged to count as a complete and consistent Eucharist? May one justify these shortcomings through pedagogical or catechetical purposes? . . . A hearing of the Word of God, the words and actions of "taking, blessing, breaking, and giving," a recalling of the Risen one in faith, a memorial of his death, resurrection, and his coming again in glory, an invocation of the Holy Spirit; these are and must remain the requisite elements of any authentic liturgy. Outside of these, one must wonder whether we are truly dealing with the Lord's Supper.*

CAN WE JUSTIFY IT?

Is this a Lord's Supper? Is this the same Lord's Supper? For the faith deposited in each of the Churches has led each to different practices, and it seems to hold true, on a first impression at least, that at least on the essential points, *Lex orandi, lex credendi,*—the faith grows out of the way we pray, as the fifth-century monk and theologian Prosper of Aquitaine put it long ago. The different Churches do not all make use of the bread and wine in the same way, notably after the Eucharistic celebration; not all require an ordained minister to preside at the celebration; not all have the same specifications for those baptized in other denominations to receive Communion from their table; and these are not simply superficial rubrics that may be easily modified, but rather practices that reveal and are deeply anchored in their faith.

All the Churches celebrate the Lord's Supper in such a way that the bread and wine, the objects of the "taking, blessing, breaking, and giving," are distributed and consumed, following Jesus's words: "Take and eat. . . . Take and drink"; but they do not all treat what remains after the distribution to those sharing in the celebration in the same way.

The East conserves the bread dipped in wine to carry it to those sick at home and for a later celebration called the "Office of the Previously Consecrated." This service does not include a Eucharistic *synaxis*, but does include Communion. In other words, the consecrated bread and wine, thus conserved, is treated with respect; the congregation bows low as the deacon crosses the church carrying those elements to the sick. However, they do not become an object of prayer or adoration; rather, Orthodox devotion has been steered toward the veneration of icons, a practice justified centuries ago by the Seventh Ecumenical Council, before the first great break between the Churches of the East and West:

> The more one looks frequently at those represented images, the more those who contemplate them will be led to recall the originals on whom they are modeled, the more they will be carried towards them; by giving them a kiss, they are showing a respectful veneration, but not an authentic adoration, which according to our faith is fitting for God alone (Second Nicea, October 13, 787).

For, in as much as Jesus Christ incarnate is the icon of the Father, he has rendered God accessible to our senses; the risk of idolatry is thereby removed. In this way, in the Orthodox tradition, devotion has been directed toward the icon, and not toward the reserved species of the Eucharist.

The Catholic West also conserves the consecrated bread for distribution to the sick (and once a year, on Good Friday, for a service of previously consecrated elements), but in this tradition the Eucharistic elements have also become objects of devotion, a practice, however, of relatively recent origin. At the beginning of the thirteenth century, at a time when the faithful rarely took Communion, the bishop of Paris commanded the host to be raised after the words of consecration so that the faithful could see it. Then, in 1229, the bishop of Liege, following visions received by St. Julienne of Mont Cornillon, instituted a feast of the Eucharist which his archdeacon, when he became Pope Urban IV, extended to the entire West in 1264. This feast of the Body of Christ (Corpus Christi), whose liturgy was composed by St. Thomas Aquinas with theological rigor, balance, and sobriety, became very popular, and a Eucharistic procession became very common towards the end of the Middle Ages. On the occasion of the "Protestant crisis," they were even more intensified. The "Forty Hours" devotion was started in 1534 in the latter part of Lent, in a spirit of repentence for sins commited during carnivals prior to Lent (this word originally signified "farewell to things of the flesh!"). This prepared the way for the "Exposition of the Blessed Sacrament" in the monstrance with short services called "Litanies to the Blessed Sacrament."

This kind of devotion can obviously give rise to abuses and thereby deflect the Eucharist from the purpose the Lord had in instituting it, specifically "Take and eat . . . ." Further, it is more than a veneration; it is intended to be an adoration. Hence, its only justifiable foundation is a faith in the real presence of Christ in the consecrated bread, an issue which is taken up in the next chapter. According to the Church's teaching, Christ is present (and thus may be adored) in the prayer of the liturgical assembly, just as he is present in his Word and in the sacraments, but "to the highest degree under the Eucharistic species," that is, under the appearances of the consecrated bread and wine (Vatican II, Constitution on the Liturgy, 7).

Thus, one should not be surprised to find in this Church a "Eucharistic devotion outside of the Mass." Whether it is valid or questionable, this devotion has produced undeniable fruits of sanctification and healing. Also, there are happenings which nourish confidence in this devotion in certain Catholic circles, and these are events that seem to have the characteristics of miracles. For example, during a fire in the church at Faverney (today Haute-Saone) in France on the Monday after Pentecost 1608, the exposed Blessed Sacrament was spared in the flames. According to the deposition given by a witness, Benigne Godichard, "the holy reliquary on which the Blessed Sacrament had been encased in a lunette had fallen back against the iron bars [the grill] separating the nave from the sanctuary. The Blessed Sacrament was suspended in the air and not held up by anything . . . since its foundation did not touch any of the iron bars." . . . The following Tuesday, during the celebration of the Mass, "this same Blessed Sacrament and reliquary descended by itself and gently came to rest on the corporal. . . ." (Manuscript of Faverney quoted by Pirolley, *The Host Saved From the Flames,* 183; Alsatia 1950).

The Reform rejected out of hand the idea that the Eucharist could be treated in any such fashion. On the Lutheran side one reads: "When, in the Papist Mass, the bread is not distributed but offered in sacrifice or locked up, carried from one side to the other, and presented for adoration, that should not be considered a sacrament" (Formula of Agreement *Solida Declaratio,* VII, 86). And Calvin was even more vehement:

> Do we have any better example of an idolatry in this world than this, to adore the gift in place of the giver? . . . They consecrate their host to carry it in procession, to expose it in splendor, to confine it in a ciborium, so that it may be adored and invoked. I ask them in what sense they believe it to be consecrated. They bring back against me the words: "This is my body." I reply to them that it is also written: "Take and eat," and I have a good reason for doing so (*Christian Institution,* XVII, IV, 36, 37).

This is because Protestants do not believe in a real presence thus localized that would remain beyond the Communion of the faithful. Even for the Communion of the sick at home, they carry out a new service. Further, what remains of the consecrated bread may be fed to the birds, the wine returned to ordinary uses or even poured down the drain. Several forms of Catholic devotion appear to them contrary to the purpose of the divine institution.

Can this opposition between Catholics and Protestants be reduced? ''What was once given as the body and blood of Christ remains something given as the body and blood of Christ, and should be treated as such'' writes a group of theologians from the two Churches belonging to the *Groupe des Dombes* (an unofficial but influential group, fifty years old now) which asks that

> from the Catholic side one recall . . . that the primary purpose of conserving the Eucharist is to distribute it later to the sick and those not present; from the Protestant side, a better manner of showing the respect due the elements that have been used in the eucharistic celebration should be put into effect, such as a later consumption, without excluding their employment for the Communion of the sick (*Towards a Common Eucharistic Faith,* 1971).

Another stumbling block between Catholics and Protestants is the question of the exercise of the ministry of presiding at the Lord's Table. Both sides agree in acknowledging here the ministry of Christ, absent physically but recognized as present through a faith similar to that manifested by the disciples on the road to Emmaus. They also agree on the role of the presider; this person takes the place of Christ, signifying thereby that the true presider of the supper is none other than Christ; this person also serves to bring about a Communion achieved through the meal between all the members of the Body of Christ.

But who may serve as this capacity as minister-presider? For the Catholic Church, such a person must be baptized and have received such power through a presbyteral ordination in a service in which the bishop, in his role as successor to the apostles, imposes hands on them. In this Church's eyes, these pastors are not themselves in a direct line from the apostles. In the eyes of Protestants, however, and even if for historical reasons the burden of ministry has not always been passed on in this fashion with historical continuity, the local pastor is no less a recipient of this Apostolic faith transmitted without interruption. The pastor also receives his ministry through an imposition of hands, about which Calvin writes: "I have no objection against this being appreciated as a sacrament, since it is a ceremony taken directly from Scripture" (*Christian Institution,* IV, XIX, 28).

Most importantly, every baptized person, because they have received the oil of priesthood, is ready for ministry; thus Calvin, who was not a priest, was never consecrated a pastor; a woman may become a pastor; and in the Churches of the reformed tradition, a lay person may be delegated by his pastor to lead the Lord's Supper. Such a practice blurs the distinction between ordained ministry and the universal priesthood.

Can this opposition be crossed, or at least narrowed? With powerful arguments the *Groupe des Dombes* mentioned above suggests a mutual recognition of ministries and suggests its own conditions for such (*For a Reconciliation of Ministries,* 1972), but will such a proposal be accepted by the Churches?

A third point of friction is that of sharing the Lord's Supper with Christians from other denominations; may a person take Communion from the table of a Church different from their own?

The Orthodox Churches have adopted a position of refusal; they do not admit a non-Orthodox to their Communion, nor do they allow an Orthodox to take Communion in a different Church. For, since the Eucharist is the sign of unity, it would give a false suggestion to indicate that unity had been achieved between the Churches. Out of mercy (they call this "the principle of economy"), very rarely they admit a non-Orthodox Christian to their table who would otherwise be deprived of the sacrament, on the condition that the person is truly in need. Along this line, in 1969 the patriarch of Moscow relaxed this rule in the case of Catholics and "Old Catholics" (another Church present in his territory), but this caused such a scandal among the other patriarchs that this decision has since been rescinded.

In this area Orthodox Christians have remained faithful to their Church's discipline. For example, here is the testimony of an Orthodox husband married to a Lutheran wife, whose children have been baptized as Protestants:

Our oldest will be confirmed in two weeks, and my heart leaps at the notion that he will finally be able to approach the Lord's table. . . . But this joy is tempered with the reminder that I will not be able to share the Lord's Supper with him or with my wife. This is not due to the absence of an invitation on the part of the Protestant Church, but rather comes entirely from my own Church, which expressly forbids me to take Communion from any other Church. But I have no intention of breaking this rule. On one level, of course, it's a question of Church discipline; but the most important reason in my eyes is that my personal satisfaction should not be given the highest priority. Rather, it is the entire community of my Church which should come to a decision on this delicate problem: Eucharistic hospitality versus Eucharistic liberty. Eucharistic hospitality consists in accepting a Christian from another Church; Eucharistic liberty consists in a Christian being permitted by his Church to take Communion with another Church. To play totally the role of a free agent here is to treat one's own community fairly shabbily. . . . But I live in hope; and I pray that one day my own Church may practice Eucharistic hospitality, even if it does not allow Eucharistic liberty until a later date. So Lord, please don't be offended if we introduce a bit of fantasy into our prayer. Because cannot take Communion currently from the same table, we transform this impossibility into a voluntary act of Eucharistic fast, in place of submitting passively to this disunion of our Churches, which is also a disunion in our personal lives; we prefer for one week to abstain from the Eucharist, in order the following week to communicate more fervently.

A Eucharistic fast of abstaining from taking Communion can be a way of making God aware of one's own suffering at not being able to take Communion from the table of another Church, especially if it is accompanied by a spiritual communion, that is, a desire to be united to God and to one's brothers and sisters in the Spirit, with the purpose of aligning oneself with the God who gives himself in the Lord's Supper. The gift which the Lord normally gives through the sacrament he can also give in an exceptional and extraordinary way outside the sacrament. During an interconfessional evangelical revival where the Lord's Supper and the Eucharist were celebrated alternatively every other day, so that on no occasion did all the participants in the revival take Communion together, two deaconesses preferred rather to practice such a fast during the entire affair.

At the other extreme, the Protestant Churches have an open policy. They admit any baptized person to their table; for it is Christ himself who invites and convokes his Church. They only hold their congregations to the necessity of the proper disposition:

> Anyone who eats the bread or takes the cup unworthily will make himself guilty before the body and blood of the Lord. Let every one examine themselves before eating this bread and drinking from this cup, for the person who eats and drinks without discernment eats and drinks their own condemnation" (1 Cor 11:27-29).

Consistently, a Protestant may then take Communion at any other Church, although the Orthodox Church will not permit this, and the Catholic Church only allows such Eucharistic hospitality by exception. However, since the Catholic Church does not easily allow its own faithful to take Communion at a Protestant Church, the more fervent among the Protestants sometimes refuse to extend such hospitality as well; rather, they expect reciprocity.

In this domain the Catholic Church honors a principle, but allows for exceptions. The principle is that one should not take Communion together unless and until the unity of the Churches is a realized fact, for such a sharing in the Eucharist is the expression of such unity. But on certain occasions it may be profitable for the faith if Christians are allowed to take Communion together; it is left to the bishop to make such a decision. Such is the doctrine and spirit of Vatican II (*Decree on Ecumenism*, 8).

In practice, except for a few bishops, such permissions have been rarely granted. But many Christians have desired to take Communion with others, and since a certain casualness about intercommunion had started to creep in, an Episcopal Commission for Unity (consisting of several bishops commissioned to monitor the ecumenical situation in France) published on March 24, 1983 an explanation of Eucharistic hospitality (*Catholic Documentation*, April 3, 1983). Unfortunately, this action upset the Reformed Church of France; for ecumenical efforts toward unity have reached the point where such a unilateral action is experienced as painfully tactless. At the same time, this clarification added nothing to the Church discipline already in effect; it merely reminded the faithful that Eucharistic hospitality could not become something customary or taken for granted, but was a matter only for exceptional cases.

These exceptions fall into two cases, that of the reception of Protestants at the Eucharist, and of the participation by Catholics at a Protestant Lord's Supper, both cases under the decision of the bishop. In the first case, the explanation asks that the Protestant should have a spiritual desire, a fraternal bonding, a respect for the Catholic faith, and participate in efforts toward unity. In the second case, it requires that the Catholic "have discovered, through a careful examination of conscience, important reasons that compel them, in this particular case, to participate in the the Lord's Supper." It warns such a person that "this participation should not be viewed as similar to the bond between the Eucharist and membership in the Church, especially in what concerns the understanding of ministry." It puts upon the person the obligation to protect themselves against any denial of their Catholic faith or of giving scandal to others. On the positive side, and for the first time in this kind of a Church document, this explanation clearly and explicitly mentions cases of mixed Church gatherings and ecumenical groups.

On the spectrum between a completely open altar and a blanket refusal, the position of the Catholic Church, at once clear in its principle and supple in its applications, is perhaps among the more successful at both preserving the Churches from an unhealthy confusion and yet goading them onward toward conversion on the road to unity.

———

SUMMARY: *In what concerns questions of Eucharistic practice, who may preside at the Lord's Supper, and who may communicate from the same table, the various Churches have different customs, all founded on convictions of faith.*

———

SEPARATED—HOW FAR?

Throughout the preceding chapters, various alternative interpretations of the unique Word of God have been indicated, which are the source of the disagreement between the Churches on the topic of the Lord's Supper. Thus, when Jesus says "This is my body. . . ." or "My flesh is real food. . . .," what meaning should we give to this Eucharistic presence and nourishment? On the other hand, when the Eucharistic prayer uses the word "sacrifice" instead of "offering," how should we understand this exactly? Also the connection of cause to effect between Communion in the same Body of Christ and the building up of the Church is understood differently by the different Churches. In short, there are many disagreements on these fundamental questions; what are the reasons for them? Are they still relevant today? To what extent are the Churches today still separated?

First, what kind of presence are we talking about when Christ offers himself in the Lord's Supper? This is a question which has been conceived differently at various times in its history. At the beginning, the Eucharist was purely and simply tradition: "This is what I have received from the Lord, and what I passed on to you" (1 Cor 11:23). In the first centuries reflection led to the recognition of the Eucharist as a symbol: the bread and wine are real in themselves, but they carry and transmit another reality which is indeed mysterious: "The bread, the fruit of the earth, receives the invocation of God and henceforth is no longer ordinary bread but the Eucharist, composed of two things, one earthly and the other heavenly," writes St. Irenaeus around the year 180 (*Against Heresies*, IV, 18, 5). The Eastern tradition has confined itself to this affirmation of faith, seeing the mysterious presence as not susceptible to further speculation. However, the Western tradition has studied this truth of divine revelation with all the resources of reason in an effort to better grasp the nature of this presence of Christ in the sacrament of the Eucharist.

The conviction has always existed that the sacramental nourishment is different from ordinary nourishment and that, as a consequence, some sort of change takes place in the course of the liturgy. The Reformers too share this notion; Calvin writes: "What they (the ancient theologians) say is that, in consecrating the bread, a secret conversion takes place, so that there is something else than the bread and wine. . . . What the ancient doctors say is true" (*Christian Institution*, IV, XVII, 14). But the investigation into the nature of the change we are talking about, and which began early, tended to set up an opposition between two extreme possibilities: either the real presence is concrete and, at its limit, material, or it is spiritual, and at its extreme, merely mythic. What became of the Eucharistic mystery out of all this? Towards the end of the eleventh century, recourse was made to the notion of substance; and, helped by the rediscovery of the works of the ancient philosopher Aristotle, the great theologians of the twelfth and thirteenth centuries finally arrived, after a long process, at a doctrine that could reconcile the opposing aspects of the situation.

Today we mean by substance that out of which a thing is made; the substance of bread is to be composed of wheat and other ingredients, just as that of a table is to be made of wood or of a pen to be made of plastic. However, Aristotle understood something else by this word that permitted him to distinguish two elements in a body: its substance and, let us say, its appearance. In bread the latter are its dimensions, its color, its form, and also (this is important) its chemical composition starting from the wheat and the other ingredients, while its substance is to be bread. This word "substance" is thus understood in a different sense, one beyond the physical—one would say then in a "meta-physical" sense. Armed with such a philosophical instrument, a theologian like Thomas Aquinas could teach that in the Eucharist there was a complete ("substantial") change from the bread and wine into the Body and Blood of Christ which had nothing to do with its appearances: this change was called "transubstantiation."

The doctrine was already expressed in these terms at the Fourth Lateran Council: the Body and the Blood of Christ "are truly contained under the species [in Latin the word *species* means appearances] of bread and wine, the bread being transubstantiated into the body and the wine into the blood through the divine power" (IV Lateran, Decree of November

30, 1215). This was recognized all throughout the Middle Ages and was defined as an element "of faith" by the Catholic Church at the Council of Trent.

Today's theologians are perfectly aware of the true intent of this doctrine:

> The defined doctrine of transubstantiation does not purport to be a positive explication of the how of the presence of Christ. Its intent is simply to say that, on the one hand, what Christ is presenting is, in keeping with his word, his own body and not something else; on the other hand, the reality empirically experienced will still be taken, very simply, at this level, for the reality of bread, and even should be. What is called "substance" and "species" should thus be understood according to their philosophical definitions (K. Rahner and H. Vorgrimler, *Short Dictionary of Catholic Theology*, article "Transubstantiation").

Thus the importance attached to the doctrine of transubstantiation by the Catholic Church is completely subservient to the purpose it is trying to serve, specifically: to believe in the real presence. As a proof of this, the Catholic Church recognizes the authenticity of the Orthodox Eucharist, where this teaching is completely unknown. Further, Pope Paul VI recognized as legitimate another theological approach: the Creator who makes bread for physical nourishment may also ordain through the power of the Holy Spirit *this bread* set aside to be divine nourishment. The encyclical *Mysterium Fidei* (September 3, 1965) teaches that "after the consecration, the species of bread and wine acquire indubitably a new signification and a new finality," although the same document immediatly goes on to say that there is here "a new reality which is justly qualified by the adjective 'ontological' " (that is to say, relative to its being).

However, the reformers of the sixteenth century questioned the doctrine of transubstantiation. For Luther and his followers, the body of Christ and the bread may coexist in the Eucharist because of the omnipresence of Christ. This is the doctrine of "consubstantiation" or "impanation." "The doctrine that accords best with Scripture is that the bread remains bread, the word St. Paul still uses for it. . . ." (*Articles of Smalkalde*, VI).

"Just as in Christ, two distinct and unmodified natures are indissolubly united, in the same way at the Lord's Supper the earthly bread and the true natural body of Christ are present together, here on earth, in the administration of the sacrament as it was instituted" (Formula of Agreement, *Solida Declaratio*, VII, 36). Calvin would not accept that the body of Christ is localized in this fashion, but did believe in an authentic participation by the communicants in the body and blood of Christ brought about through the Holy Spirit:

> Jesus Christ assures us and seals at this table a participation in his flesh and blood, through which his life pours into us. . . . He does not present to us here an empty sign . . . but rather deploys the power of his Spirit to accomplish what he promises (*Christian Institution*, IV, XVII, 10).

This is the doctrine of pneumatological communication, which one should not, however, understand as excluding a concrete presence. As proof:

> I accept every category that may serve to express the authentic communication that Jesus Christ offers us at the table in his body and blood, that may express it, I say, in such a way that one realizes that it is not only in our thoughts or imagination that we receive these things, but that their substance is truly given to us (ibid., IV, XVII, 19).

Other reformers, however, such as Zwingli, did not retain this concrete aspect of the spiritual presence, but emphasized its aspect as a memorial: "Do this in memory of me." All this only served to further fan the flames of controversy, not only between Catholics and Protestants, who were led eventually to condemn one other, but also among Protestants.

Today, with the distance of time, it is helpful to note certain similarities and differences: Luther and Calvin reject transubstantiation; Catholics and Calvinists reject the ubiquity of Christ; Catholics and Luther assert the presence of the Body and Blood of Christ, the first under the appearances of bread and wine, the second with the bread and wine. Such observations permit us to appreciate that the formal doctrines of tran-

substantiation, of the ubiquity of Christ, and of pneumatological communication all intend, in different ways and using
different categories, to express the same truth, and that is "the
mystery of the real presence of Jesus Christ in the Eucharist."
This was the conclusion that the Working Group of the
Catholic-Lutheran Ecumenical Commission, established following Pope John Paul II's trip to Germany in 1980, came to:

> It is possible to pronounce all the essential elements of the faith
> in the Eucharistic presence without making direct use of the
> terms from the doctrinal systems that combatted each other in
> the sixteenth century. Indeed, this has already been accom-
> plished in other texts of consensus and agreement; the glori-
> fied Lord becomes present at the Supper/in his body and his
> blood handed over/in his divinity and his humanity/through
> his word and promise/offered through the bread and wine at
> the Supper/through the power of the Holy Spirit/to be taken
> up by the community" (*Are the Excommunications of the Sixteenth
> Century Still in Effect?*, *Suggestions to the Churches*, Cerf, 1989,
> 187).

Catholics, Lutherans, and Calvinists (the last through the
category of pneumatological communication) all adhere to the
mystery of the real presence of Jesus Christ in the Eucharist.
Other Churches, however, descending from such reformers
as Zwingli, do not accept this. Why? Because the Lord's words
"This is my body" are understood differently. As a matter of
fact, those who believe in the real presence understand this
to be, of course, not the physical body of Jesus (as it was before his death), but the spiritual and heavenly reality of the
Risen one, for they realize that the word "is" identifies the
"this" (the bread, the visible reality) with the "my body" (the
person of Christ, the invisible reality), as happens in the recitation of a creed, where one sensible reality refers us to some
other reality. If one does not understand the word "is" is this
way, then the "this," the bread, becomes merely a sign or
representation for the body of Christ; in this case, there is no
real presence.

We must clarify further the Catholic custom of communicating only under the species of the Eucharistic bread. The Augs-

burg Confession stipulates: "It is clear that this practice, introduced contrary to the Lord's commandment and the ancient canons, is incorrect. . . . In the same way the amputation of the sacrement is contrary to its institution by Christ" (article XXII). Introduced for practical reasons and justified by the respect due to the blood of Christ, as was explained earlier, this practice was considered by the twenty-first session of the Council of Trent as falling under the power of the Church to regulate the administration of the sacraments, bestowed on "the ministers of Christ and dispensors of the God's mysteries" (cf. 1 Cor 4:1), in line with Paul's behavior when he told the Corinthians: "For the rest, I will decide that when I come" (11:34). Moreover, the Council did not make this an absolute rule, since Pope Pius IV, to whom it left this decision, in 1564 allowed the practice in Germany of communicating under both species (a practice later stopped: in 1571 in Bavaria, in 1584 in Austria, in 1604 in Hungary, and in 1621 in Bohemia). Since that time scriptural exegetes have demonstrated that the blessings which Jesus pronounced over the bread and wine go together and form one single action. In fact, in the Acts of the Apostles (2:43; 20:7), the expression "breaking of bread" is used to designate the entire meal celebrated by the disciples. Finally today, even though it happened slowly, the Catholic Church has restored Communion under both species (Vatican II, Constitution on the Liturgy, 55; Congregation of Rites, Instruction on Eucharistic Devotion, *Catholic Documentation,* June 18, 1967). Moreover, many Protestants now concede the possibility of allowing the sick to take Communion under one species in case of necessity. What before was seen as a deviation or distortion remains so, but it has now become a minor issue.

The term "Eucharistic sacrifice" goes back to the fourth century, where it was adopted from pagan cults. Over time the Lord's Supper became the Sacrifice of the Mass, to the point where popular belief, if not theologial doctine, attributed to each Mass an autonomous efficacy. Thus the Mass was passed on to the reformers as a "meritorious work," a view which clearly contradicts the unique character of Jesus's sacrifice on the Cross. From that point on opposing positions were staked out concerning the distinction between the unique sacrifice of the Cross and the thanksgiving action of the community (which may also be called a sacrifice of praise).

The reformers' position prompted a reaction from the Council of Trent, which linked the sacrament of the body and blood of Jesus to his sacrifice on the Cross. Today, however, we understand better that, while this connection does exist, the Eucharist does not in fact repeat, and has never repeated, the sacrifice on the Cross; rather, it *realizes* it, in the sense of making it present. It is a matter neither of carrying out a new sacrifice, nor of simply gathering the fruits of the sacrifice of the Cross. It is rather for the Church the opportunity to offer back to God the gift received in the person of Jesus Christ.

As has already been said, we could replace the word ''sacrifice'' with ''offering''; still, the word ''sacrifice'' seems to liturgists of the Catholic Church to express better the connection between the Eucharistic celebration and the event of the cross. However, by transposing the offertory prayer into a blessing over the bread and wine in its most recent liturgical reform, the Catholic Church has removed the main ambiguity on this point.

The early reformers took the remission of sins as the principal fruit of the Eucharist: ''This is my blood . . . poured out for all, for the forgiveness of sins'' (Matt 26:28), a position that the Council of Trent condemned. But is this not simply based on a misunderstanding? For, if the remission of sins signifies only that Jesus is Savior through his cross, then pardon is indeed a fruit of the Eucharist. But if it means that the Christian is permanently in need (and sometimes urgently) of being reconciled and renewed, then room may be made for a sacrament of forgiveness, a need that the early Lutheran reformers themselves did not deny: ''Confession has not been abolished by our preachers. For we maintain the custom of giving the Eucharist only to those who have first confessed their sins and received absolution'' (*Augsburg Confession*, article XXV). Moreover, contemporary Catholic theology recognizes that the Eucharist contains implicitly every grace rendered explicit through the other sacraments, in particular the grace of God's forgiveness through the sacrament of reconciliation.

What about Masses for the dead? Here there is still disagreement. The Reformation did not denounce all prayers for the dead at funerals, since they are practiced to this day (*"while avoiding any efficacious ritual for the deceased,"* as the reformed liturgy of 1963 makes clear), but only the notion of a transfer or application of the "sacrifice of the Mass" to the salvation of other people living and dead. But to the extent that one recognizes that the Mass does not repeat the unique sacrifice of Christ, but rather "actualizes" it, this objection loses its basis; for there is no longer room for a Mass that would somehow gain salvation for a deceased person or for the entire community of the dead. However, there *is* place for a legitimate intercession, made in connection with the Lord's presence in the celebration of the Meal, for a brother or sister, that at their death God may not reject them for their faults, at least those that were not clearly and freely decided upon.

There remains the question of the connection between the Eucharist and ecclesial communion, which determines that of being able to share in the same Eucharist. Orthodox and Catholics hold that a condition for taking Communion together is a unity already achieved between the Churches; Protestants, on the other hand, view the Eucharist as a means to bring about such a unity. This disagreement goes back to a fundamental difference in their understanding the nature of the Church.

For Protestants, the Churches are communities whose members adhere to the Word of God. However, the true Church is universal; it is the invisible Body of Christ, whose members are known only to God. To take Communion together is thus a visible manifestation of the Church already united in Jesus Christ.

For Catholics, the Church on earth has a sacramental dimension. It is the sacrament of the invisible Body of Christ whose members are known to God alone. It makes this Body present until the end of time, just as Jesus, who was God-made-man, made present the invisible God. It is thus an extension and prolongation of the incarnation. The Eucharist, the sacrament of the Body of Christ, is the preeminent sacrament of and for the Church; she carries it forward and makes it present to each generation. That is why the celebration of the Eucharist requires a Church united by the same faith.

As for the Orthodox, they think the same way; the Eucharist structures the Church, and thus can only be shared with Christians from their own churches.

The Catholic Church thus makes a narrowing of this difference on the nature of the Church a necessary precondition for intercommunion. During the visit of Pope John Paul II to the Swiss Federation of Protestant Churches, Pastor Jornod, president of the Federation, addressed these words to his guest:

> We believe that to take Communion at separate tables is not to obey the invitation of Christ. . . . The common witness of our Churches in Switzerland would be powerfully reinforced if your Church took positive steps in the direction of Eucharistic hospitality . . . toward all those who believe, justly, that the invitation by Christ to Communion is a mark of his love for all people and that this love should not be limited by our doctrinal differences.

John Paul II responded:

> The Catholic celebration is for the Church a profession of our faith in act; a complete agreement on the faith is thus a precondition for any celebration that would be true and faithful. It does no good to send conflicting signals or to mislead people. Our entire dialogue is moving toward such a common celebration. It would not mitigate the pain of separation if we avoided the cause of this pain, which is the separation itself (*Catholic Documentation*, July 15, 1984).

This is a clear exposition of the position of both sides.

SUMMARY: *The real presence, the Eucharistic offering, and sharing at the same table are questions which still divide the Churches that descend from the Reformation from the Orthodox Churches and from the Catholic Church. However, clarifications are being worked out.*

The doctrinal positions of the Catholic, Lutheran, and Calvinist Churches on the Eucharistic presence all tend toward the same purpose: to affirm the mystery of the real presence of Jesus Christ in the Eucharist.

The celebration of the offering of the gift that God makes to us in Jesus Christ offered in sacrifice does not make the Catholic Mass a new sacrifice.

It will not truly be possible for the Churches to take Communion together until the disagreement on the nature of the Church is settled.

Conclusion

We have thus seen how a meal which Jesus conducted along ritualistic lines on the eve of his death became a liturgical celebration with a form varying according to time and place; with changing situations there have been ongoing rearrangements and innovations. Perhaps on occasion there were errors or missteps, but the continued presence and faithful activity of the Holy Spirit ensures the preservation of a tradition that is authentic and not simply a continuation of the past.

Language and culture have caused the Eastern and Western traditions to diverge. However, the Reformation of the sixteenth century, the foundation of the division between the Western Churches, brought about major differences. Our prayer is the expression of our faith: *lex orandi, lex credendi.* However, because each of these Churches is returning to its sources in the primitive liturgy, a narrowing of differences may yet result, it can be hoped, indeed not in a strict uniformity, but rather in inter-ecclesial Communion. In the pursuit of this goal, there have been remarkable and powerful precursors, such as Eugene Bersier, the first pastor of the temple of the Star in Paris, who beginning in 1874 inaugurated a Eucharistic prayer with an *epiclesis* and an *anamnesis,* which read:

> God, send your Spirit over us so that, in sharing in this bread and this cup, we may receive the body and blood of your Son. God, it is in memory of your Son, of his redemptive death and of his glorious resurrection, that we celebrate his divine sacrifice, imploring you to accept its power for the salvation for all our brothers and sisters in the faith.

Is not the tone of these texts already close to that of the so-called "Liturgy of Lima" with which the Ecumenical Council of Churches celebrated the Lord's Supper at Vancouver in 1983?

The ecumenical dialogue has also contributed to a narrowing of differences and eroded the mutual condemnations of the past. More appreciative of the faith that the other tradition expresses in its liturgy, each Church is now in a position to recognize therein its own faith as well, at least in its essentials. As a consequence, it becomes possible to celebrate the Lord's Supper in terms comprehensible and accessible to the other. During a mission of interconfessional evangelization where the Eucharist was celebrated in a mixed assembly, there were Protestants who were astonished to be able to say "Amen" to the prayers of the priest. Similarly the following day, when the Lord's Supper was celebrated in the same group, there were Catholics who were pleasantly surprised to be able to say "Amen" to the pastor's prayers. Once believers come together to hear "what the Spirit has to say to the Churches" (cf. Rev 2:29), they discover together the common invitation God addresses to them toward conversion, toward Communion, and toward evangelization; "Let all give thanks (in Greek, *eucharisties*) on behalf of all," writes the Apostle Paul; that is what is pleasing "to our Savior, who desires that all people be saved and come to a knowledge of the truth" (1 Tim 2:1-4).

Documentary Appendices

Appendix 1
Liturgy of St. Hippolytus
(early version, complete text)

THANKSGIVING

We give thanks to you, O God, for your beloved Son Jesus Christ, whom you have sent to us in these last times as the savior, redeemer, and messenger of your plan, he who is the Word inseparable from yourself, through whom you created all things and whom, in your good pleasure, you sent from heaven into the womb of a virgin and who, thus conceived, was incarnated and manifested as your Son, born of the Holy Spirit and of a virgin.

It is he who, carrying out your will and winning for you a holy people, stretched out his hands as he suffered to deliver from their sufferings those who have faith in you.

He gave himself willingly over to torment, in order to defeat death and to break the chains of the devil, to trample the gates of hell, to lead the just into the light, to establish the rule of faith, and to show forth the resurrection.

INSTITUTION NARRATIVE

Taking bread, he gave you thanks and said: ''Take, eat; this is my Body which is broken for you.''

In the same way he took the chalice saying: ''This is my blood which is poured out for you. When you do this, do it in memory of me.''

EUCHARISTIC PRAYER II
(Roman Catholic Liturgy—Extracts)
PREFACE

Father, it is our duty and our salvation, always and every-where to give you thanks through your beloved Son, Jesus Christ. He is the Word through whom you made the universe, the Savior you sent to redeem us. By the power of the Holy Spirit he took flesh and was born of the Virgin Mary. For our sake he opened his arms on the cross; he put an end to death and revealed the resurrection.

CONSECRATING EPICLESIS

Let your Spirit come upon these gifts to make them holy, so that they become for us the body and blood of our Lord, Jesus Christ.

INSTITUTION NARRATIVE

Before he was given up to death, a death he freely accepted, he took bread and gave you thanks. He broke the bread, gave it to his disciples, and said: "Take this, all of you, and eat it; this is my body which will be given up for you." When sup-per was ended, he took the cup. Again he gave you thanks and praise, gave the cup to his disciples, and said: "Take this, all of you and drink from it: this is the cup of my blood, the blood of the new and everlasting covenant. It will be shed for you and for all so that sins may be forgiven. Do this in mem-ory of me."

ANAMNESIS

Recalling thus his death and his resurrection, we offer you this bread and this chalice, giving you thanks that you have judged us worthy of standing before you and of serving you as priests.

EPICLESIS

We ask you to send your Spirit on this oblation of your holy Church. In gathering them together, give to all those who participate in these holy mysteries to so share in them as to be filled with your Holy Spirit and for the strengthening of their faith in your truth.

DOXOLOGY

So that we may praise and glorify you through your Son Jesus Christ, through whom may all glory and honor be offered to you with the Holy Spirit in your holy Church, now and forever.

ANAMNESIS

In memory of his death and resurrection, we offer you, Father, this life-giving bread, this saving cup. We thank you for counting us worthy to stand in your presence and serve you.

EPICLESIS

May all of us who share in the body and blood of Christ be brought together in unity by the Holy Spirit.

DOXOLOGY

May we praise you in union with them, and give you glory through your Son, Jesus Christ. Through him, with him, in him, in the unity of the Holy Spirit, all glory and honor is yours almighty Father, for ever and ever.

Appendix 2
The Anaphora of St. Basil (extracts)

THE WORKS OF THE FATHER

You fashioned man from the slime of the earth, you honored him with the very image of God, you placed him in a paradise of delights, in promising him, if he observed your commandments, immortality and the enjoyment of eternal goods. But he disobeyed your commandment, O true God, and, led astray through the deceit of the serpent, a victim of his own sin, he subjected himself to death. By your just judgment, he was expelled from paradise into the world, sent back to the earth from which he had been taken.

However, you prepared for them, in your Christ, salvation through a new birth, for you did not reject forever the creature which you had created in your goodness; in numerous ways you watched over it in the greatness of your mercy. You sent the prophets, you performed miracles through your saints who, in each generation, were pleasing to you; you gave the Law to assist us; you sent the angels to protect us.

THE MISSION OF THE SON

And when the fullness of times had arrived, you spoke to us in your only-begotten Son, through whom you made the universe; he is the brilliance of your glory and the image of your nature; he carries all things through his powerful word; he did not jealously protect his equality with God but, as God of all eternity, he appeared upon earth, he lived among men, he took flesh from the Virgin Mary, accepted the condition of a slave, assumed our miserable body, in order to transform us into conformity with his glorious body.

EUCHARISTIC PRAYER IV
(Roman Catholic Liturgy—Extracts)
THE WORKS OF THE FATHER

Father, we acknowledge your greatness; all your actions show your wisdom and love. You formed man in your own likeness and set him over the whole world to serve you, his creator, and to rule over all creatures. Even when he disobeyed you and lost your friendship you did not abandon him to the power of death, but helped all men to seek and find you. Again and again you offered a covenant to man, and through the prophets taught him to hope for salvation.

THE MISSION OF THE SON

Father, you so loved the world that in the fullness of time you sent your only Son to be our Savior. He was conceived through the power of the Holy Spirit, and born of the Virgin Mary, a man like us in all things but sin. To the poor he proclaimed the good news of salvation, to prisoners, freedom, and to those in sorrow, joy. In fulfillment of your will he gave himself up to death; but by rising from the dead, he destroyed death and restored life.

Just as through man sin entered the world, and through sin death, it pleased your only-begotten Son, he who was eternally at your right hand, O Father, but was born of a woman, to condemn sin in his own flesh, so that those who were dead in Adam might have life in Christ. In coming into this world, he gave us the laws of salvation, he turned us away from the errors of our idols and led us to know you, the true God. In this way he won us for himself as a chosen people, a royal priesthood, a holy nation.

He cleansed us with water and sanctified us through the Holy Spirit. He gave himself over as a ransom to death to which we were captive, sold as a consequence of sin. He descended from the cross into hell to bring all things to their fulfillment. He rose on the third day and opened the path to all flesh (it was not possible that the principle of life should be subject to corruption): he became the firstfruits of all those who were asleep, the first born from the dead, so that in all things the first right might be his. He ascended into heaven and seated himself at the right hand of your majesty, in the highest heavens, whence he will come to render to each one according to their deeds. Of his passion towards salvation he left us this memorial, which we offer before you.

ANAMNESIS

Thus we also recall, Lord, the sufferings he endured which bestow salvation, his cross which gives life, his burial in the earth for three days, his resurrection from among the dead, of his ascension into heaven, of his presence at your right hand, O Father, of his second coming in dreadful power and glory, in offering you from what belongs to you these gifts which come from you.

SENDING OF THE SPIRIT

And that we might live no longer for ourselves but for him, he sent the Holy Spirit from you, Father, as his first gift to those who believe, to complete his work on earth and bring us the fullness of grace. Father, may this Holy Spirit sanctify these offerings. Let them become the body and blood of Jesus Christ our Lord as we celebrate the great mystery which he left us as an everlasting covenant.

ANAMNESIS

Father, we now celebrate this memorial of our redemption. We recall Christ's death, his descent among the dead, his resurrection and his ascension to your right hand; and, looking forward to his coming in glory, we offer you his body and blood, the acceptable sacrifice which brings salvation to the whole world.

The People: In all things, and for all things, we sing to you, we bless you, we give you thanks, Lord, and we pray you, our God.

The Priest responds: That is why, Most Holy Master, we also who have been judged worthy to serve at your most holy altar, not out of our desserts for we have done nothing good on the earth, but because of your goodness and superabundant mercies, we dare to approach your altar, we offer the sacrament of the holy body and the sacred blood of your Christ.

EPICLESIS

We pray you and implore you, O Holy of Holies, that through your goodness and benevolence your Holy Spirit may come upon us and upon these gifts here present, that he may bless them and sanctify them, that he consecrate this bread into the precious body of our Lord and Savior, Jesus Christ— and this chalice into the precious blood of our Lord and Savior Jesus Christ—poured out for the life of the world.

May all of us who share in the one bread and the one chalice be united with one another in the communion of the one Holy Spirit, and may none among us share in the holy body and blood of your Christ to their judgment and condemnation, but may we find mercy and favor together with all the saints who have been pleasing to you since the beginning of time.

INTERCESSION

Allow us to glorify you and to acclaim with one voice and heart your adorable and marvelous name: Father, Son, and Holy Spirit, now and forever, world without end. Amen

EPICLESIS

Lord, look upon this sacrifice which you have given to your Church; and by your Holy Spirit, gather all who share this one bread and one cup into the one body of Christ, a living sacrifice of praise.

INTERCESSION

Father, in your mercy grant also to us, your children, to enter into our heavenly inheritance in the company of the Virgin Mary, the Mother of God, and your apostles and saints. Then, in your kingdom, freed from the corruption of sin and death, we shall sing your glory with every creature through Christ our Lord, through whom you give us everything that is good. Through him, with him, in him, in the unity of the Holy Spirit, all glory and honor is yours, almighty Father, for ever and ever.

Appendix 3
Anaphora of St. John Chrysostom
(early version)

PREFACE

It is right and just to sing to you, to give you thanks, to worship you everywhere that your domain reaches; for you are God, you and your only-begotten Son and your Holy Spirit. It is you who have led us from nothing into being, who after our fall raised us up again; you did not rest until you had brought us back to heaven and ushered in the kingdom to come.

For all these blessings we give thanks to you, to your only-begotten Son and to the Holy Spirit. You whom the Cherubim serve, and the Seraphin with six wings, uncountable eyes, who fly in the heavens singing, crying, and exclaiming the triumphal hymn: Holy, Holy, Holy. . . .

WORKS OF THE FATHER

We also together with them, O Master of all powers, friend of humankind, we also exclaim: You are holy, infinitely holy; holy is your Son, holy is the Spirit. You are holy, infinitely holy, and your glory is immense. You have loved the world to the point of giving your Son, the only-begotten One, so that anyone who believes in him may not die but enjoy eternal life.

INSTITUTION NARRATIVE

He who, having come, so as to accomplish all things for our sake, on the night he was handed over, took bread in his holy hands, gave thanks, blessed it, broke it, gave it to his disciples and apostles, saying:

> Take, eat; this is my body, given up for you.
> In the same way at the end of the meal he took the cup, saying:
> Drink of this all of you; this is my blood, that of the new Covenant, which is poured out for you and for all, so that sins may be forgiven.

ANAMNESIS

In memory, then, of the commandment of salvation and of all that was accomplished for us: of his cross, of his burial, of his resurrection on the third day, of the ascension into heaven, of his presence at the right hand of the Father, of his second and glorious coming, we offer these things that come from you.—We praise and bless you, Lord, and we pray to you, O our God.

EPICLESIS

Send your Holy Spirit over us, and over the gifts here present; make of this bread the precious body of Christ, and of this chalice the blood of Christ, so that they may achieve for those who share in them purification of soul, remission of their sins, communion with the Holy Spirit, the fullness of the kingdom of heaven, and confidence before you, not judgment or condemnation.

We also offer you this spiritual sacrifice for all those who have gone to rest in the faith: those whom you called first, the fathers, the patriarchs, the prophets, the apostles, the preachers, the evangelists, the martyrs, the confessors, the ascetics and those who have died in the faith; above all for our holy, most pure, most blest and glorious Lady, the Mother of God and ever Virgin, Mary.

(The anaphora concludes with an intercession for the dead and an intercession for the living.)

Appendix 4
Liturgy 1 of the Evangelical Lutheran Churches of France—extracts

EPICLESIS

Send you Holy Spirit on us, your chosen people, and fill with your power your entire Church. May this Spirit of life make for us, from these earthly foods that you have given to us, a spiritual nourishment. In this way, through this bread and wine, may we have communion with the body and blood of our Savior. . . .

INSTITUTION NARRATIVE

. . . Who, the night that he was betrayed, ate with his disciples, took bread and after having given thanks, broke it and gave it to them saying: Take, eat, this is my body (elevation of the host) which is given for you. Do this in memory of me.

In the same way after the meal, he took the cup, gave thanks, and gave it to them saying: Drink from this all of you; this is my blood (elevation of the cup), the blood of the new covenant, poured out for you and for all so that sins may be forgiven. Every time that you drink from this, do this in memory of me.

Let every creature keep silence. Let us adore the Lord. (*Silence*)

ANAMNESIS

O God, we come before you to carry out the sacred act (*celebrating the meal*) that your Son commanded us:

We announce his redemptive death,
We proclaim his glorious resurrection and ascension
and in the joyful expectation of his return, we celebrate his
sacrifice,
beseeching you to lead all people to receive its power for salvation.

INTERCESSION

For us sinners who have no other refuge than your mercy,
deign to accept the prayer of your Son in our favor.

For it is through him that you create, that you sanctify, that
you give life, that you bless and bestow all good things.

DOXOLOGY

It is through him, and with him, and in him, that to you are
given all honor and glory, O God almighty Father, in the unity
of the Holy Spirit, forever and ever. Amen.

*(The epiclesis of this Protestant liturgy is located before the insti-
tution narrative and requests the coming of the Holy Spirit on the
congregation and on the elements of bread and wine.)*

DATE DUE

GAYLORD